This book
was donated by

Robert L. Nugent, Ph.D.
1920-2012

Professor Emeritus
of Modern Languages

Director of the
James F. Lincoln Library

Armenian Poetry Old and New

A BILINGUAL ANTHOLOGY

*Compiled and translated
with an introduction by*

Aram Tolegian

Wayne State University Press
Detroit, 1979

English translation copyright©1979 by Wayne State University Press, Detroit, Michigan 48202. All rights are reserved. No part of this book may be reproduced without formal permission.

Library of Congress Cataloging in Publication Data
Main entry under title:

Armenian poetry, old and new.

   English and Armenian.
   Includes index.
   1. Armenian poetry—Translations into English.
2. English poetry—Translations from Armenian.
3. Armenian poetry. I. Tolegian, Aram.
PK8831.E3A7   891'.992'1008   79-971
ISBN 0-8143-1608-5
ISBN 0-8143-1609-3 pbk.

PERMISSIONS

   Acknowledgment is made to the following for permission to reprint:
   The Armenian Review for portions of "Original Translations from Daniel Varoujan," by Aram Tolegian, *The Armenian Review,* 1954, pp. 37-54.
   Ararat, for selections from the poetry of Daniel Varoujan, translated by Aram Tolegian, *Ararat,* Autumn, 1976, pp. 16-25.
   Twayne Publishers for selections from *David of Sassoun: Armenian Folk Epic,* translated by Aram Tolegian. Copyright©1961 by Aram Tolegian.

To my parents, Manuel and Haiganoush, who by their example early instilled in me a love for the Armenian spirit and culture, and to people everywhere whose love for poetry is the very essence of life itself.

Contents

Preface   13

Introduction   17

Sahag Bartev
    The King has Come to Earth   25

Mesrob Mashdots
    Lord of Peace   29

Anonymous, from Moses of Khoren's *History of Armenia*
    The Birth of Vahakn, King of Armenia   33
    Conception Grand and Marvelous   33
    Pillar of Light   35

Krikor Naregatsi
    Vartavar   39
    A Birthday Melody   41
    Prayer One, from the *Book of Lamentations*   43

Nerses Shnorali
    Awake   47

Frig
    Complaint   51

Konstantin Yerzengatsi
    Love Song   57

Grigoris Akhtamartsi
    Song to Weeping, and to the Owner of a
      New-built House and Garden   63

Hovhanness Telkurantsi
    Song of Love   69

Nahabed Kouchag
    Thoughts   73

Nerses Mokatsi
    Argument between the Sky and Earth   81

Nagash Hovnaton
    Song of Love 89

Psalm-reader (Tbir) Baghdassar
    Song 93

Sayat-Nova
    I'll Not Cry "Alas" 97
    The World is a Window 99

Ghevond Alishan
    Hrazdan 103

Michael Nalbandian
    Freedom 107

Mgrdich Beshiktashlian
    Spring 113

Rapael Patkanian
    Cradle Song 117
    Vartan's Song 119

Gevork Dodokhian
    Swallow 125

Raffi (Hagop Melik-Hagopian)
    Little Lake 129

Ghazaros Aghayan
    Remembrance 133

Jivani (Serop Levonian)
    They Come and Go 137

Bedros Tourian
    My Death 141

Alexander Dzadourian
    Don't Cry, Bulbul 145

Hovhanness Hovhanissian
    A Gentle Sleep 149

Hakop Hakopian
    My Land 153

Hovhanness Toumanian
    The Armenians' Grief 159
    Quatrains 159
    David of Sassoun 161

Avetik Issahakian
    From Ravenna 215
    Where Does the Stone Lie? 215
    Over the Stream 217

Vahan Tekeyan
    The Hanoum 221
    The Beautiful Ones 221

Siamanto (Adom Yarjanian)
    A Handful of Ash 225

Daniel Varoujan
    Tillers 231
    The Flickering Lamp 231
    Oriental Bath 233

Missak Metsarents
    The Hut 243

Rouben Sevak
    Why? 249

Vahan Derian
    The Gallows 253
    In the Mist 253
    Farewell Song 255

Azad Veshtouni
    The Newsboy 259

Matevos Zarifian
    Compassion 263

Yeghishe Charents
    Sun-flavored Speech 267
    Fatherland 267
    A Vision of Death 269

Nairi Zarian
    To my Native Home 273

Sarmen
    The Lamb 277
Guegham Sarian
    The Glass 281
Gourgen Mahari
    Night 285
Vagharshak Norents
    Sister 289
Soghomon Taronsti
    Old Stork 293
Vahe Vahian
    Requiem 297
Souren Vahouni
    Swallow 301
Ashod Grashi
    Ah, It Came to Mind 305
Moushegh Ishkhan
    Joined with our Land 311
Hovhanness Shiraz
    Impromptu 315
    Niagara 315
    Oak and Eagle 315
Gourgen Borian
    This Endless Journey 319
Hamo Sahian
    In the Woods 323
    Green Poplar of Nairi 325
Gevork Emin
    Siamanto's Prayer 329
    Ah, this Massis 331
Maro Markarian
    The Heights are Harmful 337
    The Size of a Heart 337

Silva Gaboudikian
    Love Songs 341
    Lilith 345

Hrachia Hovhanissian
    When the Rain Passes 349
    The Swan 349

Vahakn Garents
    For my Dreams 355
    Get Away from Your Self, Go 357

Vahakn Davtian
    My Heart 361

Aram Arman
    The Chant of the Returned Poet 365

Barouyr Sevak
    Good Evening 369
    Morning Light 369

Index of Titles and First Lines 375

Preface

Whether or not poetry truly can be translated from one language into another is an open question, but certainly there can be no exact translation. The translator knows that absolute correspondence in tone, sound, and meaning are unattainable; his reason recoils from the prospect. Yet thousands of translators, including hundreds of great poets, have put their hands to the task of translation. Whatever else may induce the translator to attempt the well-nigh impossible, there is always the hope in his heart that, fate permitting, he may achieve in the translated work a felicitous approximation of the original. A translator is like a lover: he feels he "alone has looked on beauty bare," and his enthusiasm compels him to share with others the wealth, beauty, and lyricism he has discovered in the poetry of a foreign language. Hence the present volume, an attempt to bring the traditions and genius of Armenian poetry into the mainstream of literature translated into English.

Precious little Armenian poetry has been published in English, and that little has come to us in works which first appeared at the turn of the century. It is my hope that this volume, in modern English and chronologically arranged, will fill a large gap for both the general reader and the specialist. For the universities and colleges in the United States now offering Armenian studies programs and the Armenian schools which have recently initiated Armenian language and literature studies, this bilingual anthology may provide a useful text.

The reader who knows Armenian will observe that a first line title is routinely supplied for the Armenian text where a title was not assigned by the poet or by convention; for the English translation I have in some instances preferred to use a short descriptive title. A complete index of titles and first lines accompanies the English translation. Punctuation, except in those few modern poems in which it was clearly the poet's intention that it serve an extraordinary function, here follows the standard practice of English. Line lengths and stanzaic forms in the translations are as consistent with the Armenian originals as the stylistic and formal differences between the two traditions will allow. In several of the earlier poems, indentation of lines or an asterisk seemed to me useful shorthand ways of indicating to readers abrupt shifts in subject or tone, characteristic of an ancient and foreign tradition, which might otherwise have been momentarily confusing. It is certain that some readers' favorite poems have been omitted from this anthology, but only so much can be put between the covers of a book. As the anthologist, I am ultimately responsible for the judgments on what to include and what to omit. I believe that the poems in this anthology represent the full range of Armenian poetry.

Throughout this work I have been guided by one principle: the translated poem must sound like, and *be* like, the poem in its original language. Often the exact word could be found, but was discarded in favor of another if the change improved the poem in English. Yet it is also proper to indicate that I strove for as much literalness as two non-cognate languages would allow. Again, readers familiar with Armenian will be tempted perhaps to compare translated lines with original lines and will doubtless find a word here, a phrase there, not in consonance with his ideas. What they will find in the pages to follow is my own laborious resolution of the innumerable difficulties of translation, among them the yoking of both music and meaning to a new language. Readers who do not know Armenian can, I hope, simply enjoy these translations as poems. And it is my hope that this anthology, the product of a lifetime love for some of the world's best poetry, will have a special place in those homes in which a regard for poetry is well and truly nourished.

I am greatly indebted to Berj Mesrobian, Senior Research Fellow of the Armenian Academy of Sciences and chairman of the English Department, Valery Brussov Institute of Foreign Languages, Yerevan, Armenia, for his aid, his poetic insights, and his unwavering enthusiasm for this project from its inception to the present, a period of some eight years. During this time our massive correspondence was pleasantly interrupted by two face-to-face work sessions, one in Armenia and one in the United States.

I also acknowledge most gratefully the many kindnesses of Barkev Mardirosian, Section Head of the (Armenian) Committee for Cultural Relations with Armenians Abroad. Mr. Mardirosian has graciously responded to my many requests, including those for photographs of the poets, typescripts in the original Armenian of poems submitted for translation, and a blanket release of copyright claims. Through his generous efforts I was able to work with, and benefit from the counsel of, a committee of poets in Armenia: Vahakn Davtian, Maro Markarian, and Silva Gaboudikian. I owe them special thanks for helping to select many of the poems included in this anthology; I prize their collective insights and cherish their judgments. I am greatly indebted as well to Arazi Tirabian, Head Librarian, Miasnikyan National Armenian Library, for providing me with authoritative, standard edited texts of all the poems included here. Without his generous support I would have been reduced to working with out of print or unedited texts. Through the years I have sought and received the advice and counsel of many friends, too numerous to acknowledge properly in this space, but I do want to give special thanks to Gilbert Chorbajian of Los Angeles, who for a period of thirty years has shared my enthusiasm for Armenian poetry and given generously of his time and energy to advance the progress of this work. I acknowledge with thanks the generous financial assistance of Archie H. Dickranian which has helped to defray the cost of the publication of this book.

I am also deeply grateful to Wendy Wienner of the Wayne State University Press for her many helpful suggestions and for the quality of her poetic insights during the final editing of the anthology. I found her to be a poet as well as an editor.

Finally, I acknowledge a very heavy obligation indeed to the Committee for Cultural Relations with Armenians Abroad, whose president, Vartkes Hamazaspian, has consistently given this project broad and generous administrative support.

Aram Tolegian
Monterey Park, California

Introduction

By edict of her king, Armenia converted to Christianity in A.D. 301. A century later, in 406, the Armenian alphabet was invented. These two events had immeasurable significance for Armenian literature and culture. The introduction of Christianity meant an abrupt end to the old pagan culture, for Christian zealots destroyed the ancient idols, the temples with their ceremonial inscriptions, literary works and chronicles. What little ancient poetry survived the storms and drifts of time was transcribed in the work of later writers. The fifth century Armenian historian Moses of Khoren quotes brief passages from the legends "Haik and Bel," "Ara the Beautiful and Semiramis," "Tigranes and Azhdahak," and "Artashes and Artavazd" (the former two dating from the second millennium and the latter two from the second century B.C., respectively), and so preserves a flavorful but pitifully meager bit of the old poetry. The anonymous poets whose work Moses of Khoren records represent what must have been a rich and cultured poetic tradition. But with Christianity began new poetic traditions, and with the creation of the alphabet the time had come for poetry to be written in Armenian.

Before Mesrob Mashdots invented the Armenian alphabet Armenians had used Greek and Syriac characters; though their language was fully developed, they had never possessed their own alphabet. The rapid adoption of the new alphabet created the ideal environment for a new Armenian literature. Fifth century historians and chroniclers turned away from Greek and wrote almost exclusively in Armenian. The Armenian church accomplished the monumental task of translating the Bible from the Greek. Although Armenian literature had become markedly more secular as the ferment of the early Christian period subsided, one of the major developments in Armenian poetry, the *sharakan*, was religious in character. The first *sharakans* (chantable religious poems, associated with church ceremonies) were written by

Some of the material in this introduction has been condensed from an unpublished full-scale literary and historical essay by Professors Mkrdich Mekerian and Karnig Ananian of Yerevan, Armenia. Limitations of space regrettably prevented its inclusion in this book, for which it was originally intended.

Mesrob Mashdots, and both their form and their beauty influenced generations of Armenian poets. Indeed, before the end of the fifth century a huge mass and variety of literature had been produced, some of great quality: the period is known as Armenia's Golden Age.

From the seventh to the eleventh centuries the Arabs repeatedly invaded Armenia, subjugating the people and exacting tribute. In the middle of the ninth century, however, the Armenians were able to establish their independence, and the struggles leading to that victory produced a cycle of epics known collectively as the "David of Sassoun." In 1875 Bishop Karekin Servantziants became the first scholar to publish part of the material under the title *David of Sassoun;* since that time folklorists have transcribed from the recitals of storytellers over one hundred variants of the epic. But it is in Hovhanness Toumanian's spirited "David of Sassoun" that the central hero of the epic, David, is first made a symbol of the aspirations and anxieties of his people, whose wishes he fulfills by restoring peace, regaining for them their lost liberties, and preserving their dignity and identity as an ancient Christian people.

Not only the Arabs but the Byzantines, Turks, Mongols, and Persians invaded Armenia and wasted her cities and countryside. As a direct consequence of these wars and the ensuing turmoil, the task of guarding and maintaining cultural traditions fell to the Armenian church. Monastic institutions, perhaps even more than in early medieval Europe, now quite literally became islands of civilization. They were centers of learning as well as repositories of culture: the monks copied, translated, created, and preserved. The tenth century religious leader and poet Naregatsi, for example, drew on earlier traditions, such as the *sharakan*. Partly as a result of his writings, the tenth century saw an enormous upsurge of interest in both religious and secular poetry; indeed, generations of readers and poets have been intrigued by both his technical accomplishments and his highly evocative style. Two centuries later another religious figure, Shnorali ("The Gracious One"), wrote poetry that was to be a significant influence on the trend toward secular lyrics.

From the thirteenth through the eighteenth centuries Armenia suffered a series of appalling calamities, struggling continuously against foreign rule and feudal plunder. The struggle itself contributed to an accelerating production of secular poetry, for secular poetry tended to accept the world as it actually was. In the thirteenth century began a new phase in the history of Armenian literature, highlighted by the rise of Middle Armenian. Secular poetry was now written in Middle Armenian, the vernacular, while Grabar, Old Armenian, which had been long dead as a spoken language, remained in use only among historians and religious authors. Having left aside religious topics, then, poets were free to evaluate the quality of life in the "real" world, to weigh the chances for human happiness, to consider love afresh. Lyricism became the dominant poetic mode, replacing the earlier conventions of mysticism, and in lyrics the poets wrote not only of love and passion but of injustice and inequality among men. An apparently indigenous humanism developed, side by side with an all-pervading skepticism. The church became more liberal and national in character during this period; many of the poets were schooled in monasteries. But the course of poetry had veered away from the religious ruminations of the earlier age and returned only in isolated instances to the themes of supplication and sin, absolution and redemption.

Theology has an uncertain place, for example, in Frig's dry observation that

> One is descended from a wealthy lord,
> Another, on his father's side, a bum;
> One owns a thousand mules and horses,
> Another owns neither goat nor kid.

Forsaking heaven, Yerzengatsi glorifies the sun as the creator of all that is good and beautiful; he and the other poets who sense the conflict between spiritual purity and bodily desires resolve the issue, sometimes a bit uneasily, in favor of love. Telkurantsti, in fact, seeks immortality through love, while Akhtamartsi declares that his beloved can work more wonders than "the mighty cross." Others in this period wrote patriotic songs and songs of exile, and a poet of rather classical bent, Psalm-reader (Tbir) Baghdassar, was the first to see his poems in print. Still, the most prominent poet of the age was Hovnaton, whose poetry is rich with love and satire and full of songs in praise of wine and merry-making.

If Hovnaton was the most prominent of the age, however, Sayat-Nova is the most enduringly popular. By common consent the quintessential troubadour, many of his poems are still sung by Armenians everywhere. True to the tradition of the troubadours, his poetry is filled with songs of love—often, unrequited love. Sayat-Nova uses a wide range of poetic devices and an easy, frequent scattering of words from the languages of neighboring countries. His handling of Persian, Georgian, Kurdish, Azerbaijani, and Turkish words and phrases is so deft that their appearance in his poems seems quite natural (and yet causes translators much difficulty); these words in fact impart a distinctive folk quality. Readers are made to feel comfortable by his use of dialect, and seem to enter readily into his stories of love, pain, and simple affirmation.

After the Russo-Persian War of 1827 eastern Armenia came under Russian rule. Russia was culturally and economically far more advanced than Turkey and Persia, which were mired in feudal backwardness. The Armenians prospered under Russian authority, for they had a Christian environment which provided them with schools and a modicum of freedom. Further, eastern Armenia had always had close cultural ties with Russia, so the Russian presence did not seem unduly strange. It was at this time that Armenian literature began the journey from the medieval to the modern age. The guiding spirits were Alishan in the west and Abovian in the east. Both were deeply concerned with bringing about a national revival and an appreciation of the various liberation movements. Alishan, in his poetry, championed the struggle for liberation from Turkey; Abovian, in his 1840 novel, laid the foundations for a modern Armenian literature and a modernized vernacular. Together they prepared the way for modern Armenian poetry.

By the mid-nineteenth century, poetry had emerged as Armenia's dominant literary form, and it was through their poetry that writers of both eastern and western Armenia voiced the people's fears, and their desire for freedom. Among these new poets were Nalbandian and Tourian. Nalbandian, a teacher and a dedicated revolutionary, allied himself with Russian political authors such as Herzen and Chernyshevsky in the battle against czarism. The ideals of the French Enlightenment inform his poetry, and his portrayals of everyday Armenian life brought a newly realistic element to Armenian poetry. While Tourian also wrote powerful poems of social injustice, his best poems sing of love and nature. He often depicts those brief moments in which we are released from life's tragedy and strife and allowed to enter an idyllic world of romantic love.

At the turn of the century Toumanian, Varoujan, and Siamanto, among others, were writing. These artists, in Armenia as elsewhere, were conscious of their art and themselves as artists, as never before. The Armenian poets all turned to their native language with a fresh curiosity and a desire to investigate its possibilities, but they worked in many different poetic forms, from traditional to free verse, and on a number of subjects. Toumanian, Armenia's greatest folklore poet, explored the temperament of his people. He created individual voices for the characters of folk legends, and then blended these in a song of national aspiration. Less topical than Siamanto, Varoujan, and many others writing in those tragic times, Toumanian recaptured Armenia's heritage and released its living spirit.

Siamanto (Adom Yarjanian) and Varoujan both wrote directly of the horrors they had known—the Armenian massacres of 1894-96, the carnage at Adana in 1909, and other bloody consequences of the Ottoman Empire's policy of exterminating Armenians. Siamanto's poetry, though filled with epic denunciation and anguish, urged the will to fight and hope; Varoujan's poems told of Armenian rural life and of the ancient and medieval worlds as well as political outrage. Both Siamanto and Varoujan died in the Turkish genocide of 1915—as well as an entire society.

In 1920 Soviet power was established in Armenia, and this signaled yet another era in Armenia's history and culture. Armenian literature became an integral part of the Soviet multinational literature, maintaining its national character and traditions, however, in its new socialist age. Proletarian literature was a natural outgrowth of the new society, but Hakopian and others had already set the tone and partially indicated the scope of poetry in the proletarian spirit, in the first decade of the century. The proletarian writers stressed the working man's energy and his ability to remake society; they concentrated on those gathering social forces which could carry out a new and historic mission. Poets wrote with the belief that society is perfectible, for Armenia's proletarian society (like any society in the aftermath of a revolution) was hopeful, aspiring to shake off past evils and embrace a shining future. So, during the twenties, Charents accepted the socialist schema for a new order. He perceived revolutionary socialism to be the only road to salvation for a small country, and much of his poetry from that period is a ringing call to his countrymen to participate in the new life. His work in new literary forms continued, but as time passed his poetry became increasingly nostalgic and lyrical. Some of his best work has this reflective character. Still, perhaps his greatest contribution to Armenian poetry was throwing off the preoccupation with sorrow and finding the pulse of the new age.

The thirties and forties saw the scope of poetry greatly enlarged. Younger voices mixed with the older, and the past found a place alongside the present and future. World War II conjured up the sad and inevitable themes of war, but during the last two years of the war the range of lyricism widened markedly, as poets probed deeply into the more private human emotions. The intimate lyric, the lyric of the soul's depth and the mind's contour, appeared everywhere. Gaboudikian, for example, captures not only the spirit of public concerns but the hidden spirit as well, in frank yet delicately wrought confessionals; Davtian blends subtle perceptions of the human soul with the traditional materials of the native literature. Markarian's poetic monologues, though intimate, reverberate for the reader until they seem the reader's own voice.

Writers in other traditions include Sahian, Emin, and Barouyr Sevak. Sahian meditates on the relationship of man and nature and how harmony between the two can be achieved. Emin's poetry is suffused with the life and spirit of Armenia: sorrowful tales of the past and present spoken by a prophet concerned and yet hopeful about the future. Finally, in this brief sketch of Armenia's literary history, we come to Barouyr Sevak. Sevak's work is quite different from that of his contemporaries. Analytical examinations of life, his poems investigate social issues and mores, the accepted notions of life. With his free, uneven lines he ranges over ideas, excising and subtly recombining their elements in a new synthesis. And Armenia's literature itself, like any literature, is a synthesis—of history and individual genius, of destructions and creations.

And, perhaps like every other ancient civilization, Armenia took poetry as its first mode of literary expression. In whatever age, whatever straits, she has continued to create poetry, and though scattered across the world, Armenians generally know and revere their poets. The recitations of small children, the recitations at public gatherings and meetings, the jubilees organized to honor their poets all attest to the regard Armenians have for their poetic heritage. In Armenia her living heritage, her living poets, command both affection and respect. Perhaps there is something in the Armenian's spirit that compels him to make poetry of experiences and events. Perhaps the travail of centuries, the massacres and deportations, the persecutions and deprivations, as well as the great and noble in his history and traditions, have transfused his spirit in such a way that every Armenian feels himself, to some degree, a poet.

Սահակ Պարթեւ
Sahag Bartev
348–439

Թագաւոր Գոլով Քո Յաշխարհ

Թագաւոր գոլով քո յաշխարհ,
Մտեր ի քաղաքն Երուսաղէմ,
Նստեալ ի վերայ հողեղէն նոր յաւանակի,
Կոչել զՀեթանոսս յերկրպագութիւն։

Մերքն ոստովք ձիթենեօք,
Եւ տղայքն ոստովք արմաւենեօք
Եւ երամ-երամ դասուքն ադադակէին՝
Ովսաննա՛, օրհնեալ եկեալ ի յանունն Տեառն։

Ցնծացաւ սուրբ Սիովն,
Բերկրեցան սուրբ եկեղեցիք.
Եւ խնդութեամբ բացմաւ՝ ելին ընդ առաջ,
Օրհնէին զգալուստ քո, փրկիչ, յաշխարհ։

The King has Come to Earth

The King has come to earth,
And seated on a young ass
He enters Jerusalem,
Calling the pagans to prayer—

The children come with palm branches,
The elderly come with olive branches,
The people shout with one voice
"Glory, blessed be the name of the Lord."

Holy Zion rejoices,
Delight fills the holy Churches—
All come to meet You joyously,
Blessing Your arrival, O Savior of this world.

Մեսրով Մաշտոց
Mesrob Mashdots
361–440

Վտամգիմ ի Բազմութենէ
Մեղաց Իմոց

Վտանգիմ ի բազմութենէ մեղաց իմոց,
Աստուած խաղաղութեան, օգնեա՛ ինձ։

Ալեկոծիմ հոգմով անօրէնութեան իմոյ,
Թագաւոր խաղաղութեան, օգնեա՛ ինձ։

Ի խորս մեղաց ծովու տարաբերեալ ծփիմ,
Նաւապետ բարի, փրկեա՛ զիս։

Lord of Peace

O Lord of Peace, help me to turn away
From the many sins that threaten me.

O Lord of peace, keep me away from lawlessness,
Which buffets me as the waves.

O good Helmsman, save me from the depths of sea-deep sin,
On which I float like an abandoned raft.

Անանուն, Մովսէս Խորենացի
Հայոց Պատմութիւն գործէն

Anonymous, from Moses of Khoren's
History of Armenia
fifth century

Վահագնի Ծնունդը

Երկնէր երկին, երկնէր երկիր,
Երկնէր եւ ծովն ծիրանի.
Երկն ի ծովուն ունէր եւ զկարմրիկն եղեգնիկ.

Ընդ եղեգան փող ծուխ ելանէր,
Ընդ եղեգան փող բոց ելանէր,
Եւ ի բոցոյն վազէր խարտեաշ պատանեկիկ.

Նա հուր հեր ունէր,
Բոց ունէր մօրուս,
Եւ աչկունքն էին արեգակունք։

Խորհուրդ Մեծ Եւ Սքանչելի

Խորհուրդ մեծ եւ սքանչելի,
Որ յայսմ աւուր յայտնեցաւ,
Հովիւքն երգեն ընդ հրեշտակս՝
Տան աւետիս աշխարհի։

Ծնաւ նոր արքայ
Ի Բեթղեհէմ քաղաքի,
Որդիք մարդկան, օրհնեցէ'ք,
Զի վասն մեր մարմնացաւ։

Անբաւելին երկնի եւ երկրի
Ի խանձարուրս պատեցաւ,
Ոչ մեկնելով ի հօրէ՝
Ի սուրբ այրին բազմեցաւ։

The Birth of Vahakn, King of Armenia

The sky is turbulent, turbulent the earth,
Turbulent the purple sea,
And turbulent also the red reed in the sea.

Smoke curled out of the reed,
Flame leaped out from the reed,
And out of the reed a fair child came forth.

His hair glowed,
His beard flamed,
And his eyes were very suns.

Conception Grand and Marvelous

Conception grand and marvelous
That was revealed today—
The shepherds sing with angels
And bring good tidings to the world.

A new King is born
In the village of Bethlehem:
O sons of man, bless Him
Who for our sake became flesh and blood.

The infinite One of heaven and earth
Is cradled here in a manger,
Without leaving His Father
The holy Child lies here, enthroned.

The Birth of Vahakn. This is the full text given by the historian. He represents it to be a song, and a fragment of a longer work.
His beard flamed. Vahakn is a mythic, legendary god-king. His birth is here treated supernaturally, hence, though born a child, he is endowed with attributes of manhood.

Սիւն Լուսոյ

Սիւն լուսոյ եւ ամպ հովանի, սուրբ կոյս,
Որ ցոյցեցեր ի մեզ զցօղն երկնային,
զքեզ բարեբանեմք, Աստուածածին եւ կոյս։

Անկէզ մորենի եւ սրովբէ հողեղէն, սուրբ կոյս,
Քանզի պտուղն կենաց ի քէն տուաւ մեզ,
զքեզ բարեբանեմք, Աստուածածին եւ կոյս։

Անիծից լուծիչ եւ քաւիչ մեղաց, սուրբ կոյս,
Որ զանտանելին էից ի գիրկս քո բարձեր,
զքեզ բարեբանեմք, Աստուածածին եւ կոյս։

Pillar of Light

O holy virgin, pillar of light, cloud of shade,
Thou who bedewed us with heavenly grace,
Come let us praise thee, divine virgin, mother.

O earthly divinity, O divine tree made fruitful,
Thou gave us the fruit of thy life.
Come let us praise thee, divine virgin, mother.

Releaser of curses, amender of sins,
Thou who accepts sinners with wide-open arms,
Come let us praise thee, divine virgin, mother.

Գրիգոր Նարեկացի
Krikor Naregatsi

tenth century

Վարդավառին

Գոհար վարդն վառ առեալ
  ի վեհից վարսիցն արփենից։
Ի վեր ի վերայ վարսից
  ծաւալէր ծաղիկ ծովային։
Ի համատարած ծովէն
  պղպջէր գոյնն այն ծաղկին,
Երփին երփնունակ ծագկին
  շողշողէր պտուղն ի ճղին։
Քրքում վակասիր պտուղն
  սնանէր խուռն տերեւով.
Տերեւն տալիգ տուողին
  գոր երգէր Դաւիթ Հրաչային։
Ի փունջ խուռներամ վարդից
  գոյնզգոյն ծաղկունք ծաղկեցան։
Այդ սոս ու տոսախ ծառերդ
  վարդագոյն ոստս արձակեցին։
Այդ նոճ ու բողբոջ արոսդ
  գարդ առեալ վարդն շուշանին.
Շուշանն շողէր հովտին,
  շողշողէր դէմ արեգականն.
Այն Հիւսիսային հովէն
  հով հարեալ գոհար շուշանին.
յԱյն հարաւային լեռնէն
  քաղցր օդով ցօղէր շուշանին։
Շուշանն շաղով լցեալ,
  շող-շաղով եւ շար մարգարտով։
Մաղկունքդ ամէն շաղ առին,
  շաղն յամպէն, ամպն յարեգակնէն.
Աստեղեդ ամէն շուրջ առին,
  դէմ լուսնին գունդ-գունդ բոլորին։
Գունդ-գունդ խաչածեւ գնդակ,
  յօրինուած երկնից շուրջանակ։
Փառք Հօր եւ Որդւոյն յաւէտ,
  սուրբ Հոգւոյն այժմ եւ յաւիտեանս։

Vartavar

The misted rose has drawn a veil
    Against the bold rays of the sun.
Above, on the sun's rays,
    The seaborn flower spreads.
From the vast ocean
    Shines the flower's bright color,
And in the branches shimmer
    The fruits of the splendid flower,
The golden ripe fruit
    Protected by the leafy denseness,
The harp-shaped leaf
    Sung by David the Wondrous.
In the bouquet of many-hued roses
    Blooms a rainbow of vivid buds,
And in the cypress and poplar trees
    Life-flushed branches move free,
And among the cypress shoots
    The rose blossoms out and tints the lily.
The lily shimmers against the sun—
    The northern breeze
Fans the gem-like lily,
    The sweet air from the southern hills
Gently dews the lily—
    The lily is laden with dew,
With soft and beaming rays.
    All the flowers glow with dew,
As the dew from the clouds, the clouds from the sun.
    Drifts of clustered stars
Circle, as balls around the moon—
    Ball upon ball, cross-shaped clusters of balls
Shape a compass fashioned in the heavens.
    Glory to Father and Son forever,
To the Holy Spirit, now and through all time.

Vartavar, literally "Flaming Rose," was a pagan festival in honor of Anahit, goddess of chastity, founder of races, and protector of the Armenian people. After the Armenians adopted Christianity Anahit's festival became in time the Feast of the Transfiguration of Christ.
David the Wondrous, the biblical David who slew Goliath.

Մեղեդի Ծննդի

Աչքն ծով ի ծով ծիծաղախիտ
    ծաւալանայր յառաւօտուն,
    երկու փայլականաձեւ արեգական նման.
    շողն ի ժմին իջեալ յառաւօտէ լոյս:
յԱյտէն նռնենի սարդիատունկ
    գեղաշիտակ ծայրից ծագկանց,
    որոյ սիւնն ի սրտին նուսխայօրէն
    կարկաճայր սաթբերունի սէր:
Ձեռացն եղիշոյ կամարակապ կապեր,
    ատիճագ պատիճագ, ստղի խտղի երգով:
Հիւսէր գելելեյան ընդ մէմեանս,
    հանդարտոտիկ խաղայր, թիւնէթեկին ճեմէր:
Բերանն երկթերթի, վարդն ի շրթանց կաթէր.
    լեզուին շարժողին քաղցրերգանայր տալիղն:
Ի ծամին խեղեկին հագրէ գի նոյն սէր
    հոգիազգեստեալ գեղն ի գինւոյն գոյն:
Վարսիցն երամից գարդ, երամից գարդ,
    ուրոյս են առեալ եռահիւսակն բոյորեալ այտիւք:
Մօցն լուսափայլ, կարմիր վարդով լցեալ,
    ծգիքն ծիրանի մանուշակի հոյլք:
Խնկեալ ի կնդրկէ բուրվառ հրով ասաուածայնով լցեալ.
    ճայն քաղցրանուագ, որ ի նմանէ Հնչէր:
Գեղեցիկ պատմուճանան գարդարեալ էր,
    ի կապուտոյ, ի ծիրանոյ, ի բեհեզոյ, ի յորդանէ
    ոսկեղողէր գոյնն:
Գօտին արծաթափայլ ոսկէտուտուն,
    կամարակապ յականց, յականց շափիւղայ,
    մանրամասին յօրինուածով պճնեալ:
Անճինն ի շարժել մարգարտափայլ գեղով,
    ուտիցն ի գնալ շողն ի կաթել առնոյր:
Այն թագաւորին, այն նորածին փրկչին,
    գքեզ պասակողին փառք յաւիտեանս․ ամէն:

A Birthday Melody

Her eyes gaze
>   Over the sparkling morning sea
>   Like two bright orbed suns,
>   While the dew settles from the dawn.

Her pomegranate-hued cheeks are like flowers,
>   And elegant as the laurel plant
>   Through whose stem
>   Blooming love whispers to the flower's heart.

Her smooth arms arched over her head, she sings
>   Sweetly, pleasingly, harmoniously;
>   Ever weaving melody into melody,
>   She moves calmly, with a splendid gait.

Her mouth, fashioned as two leaves, spills roses from its lips,
>   Her tongue is tuneful as a harp;
>   Her braided beautiful hair, adorned with rosemary,
>   Takes on the dark hue of life-giving wine.

Her lovely hair, her lovely thrice-plaited hair,
>   Ever tenderly frames her face.
>   Her bright bosom is strewn with red roses,
>   Her wrists garlanded with sprays of purple violets.

With a holy fire, the censer gives up its perfume,
>   Its chains echoing melodious sounds.
>   She is dressed in a shimmering cloak—
>   Lovely, blue, gem laced, and golden—
>   In a tunic brilliant with gold.

Her belt of shining silver, edged with gilt,
>   Sapphire encrusted, was worked into arabesques;
>   When she moves, her motions are bright;
>   Light sparkles around her feet.

To that King, to that newborn Savior,
>   To Him who adorned thee, glory forever, Amen.

Մատեան Ողբերգութեան
—Բան Առաջին—

(Հատուած)

Ձայն Հառաչանաց
Հեծութեան սրտի՝
Ողբոց աղաղակի
Քեզ վերընծայեմ, տեսողդ գաղտնեաց.
Եւ մատուցեալ եղեալ
Ի հուր թախծութեան
Անձին տոչորման՝
զՊտուղ ըղձից ճենճերոյ սասանեալ մտացս,
Բուրվառաւ կամացս
Առաքել առ քեզ։
Այլ Հովտոտեսցիս Հայեցիս, գթած,
Քան ի պատարագն բոլորապտուղ
Մատուցեալ ծխոյն բարդութեան։
Ընկալ գտակաւամասնեայ բանիցս յօդուած։
Քեզ ի Հաճութիւն,
Եւ մի' ի բարկութիւն.
Ելցէ ի խորոց աստի
Զգայութեանց խորհրդակիր սենեկիս
Վաղվաղակի ժամանել առ քեզ՝
Կամաւորական նուէր բանական գոհիս,
Ողջակիզեալ գօրութեամբ ճարպոյ՝
Որ յինն է պարարտութիւն։

Prayer One, from the *Book of Lamentations*

A word with God from the depths of my heart

Sounds of lamentation,
Groans from my heart,
These I offer up to Thee,
Almighty God.
From the incense burner
Of my soul
I offer up to Thee
The burnt ashes
Of my soul's vagrant desires,
The fiery sorrow that torments me.
O merciful God, please,
Before the fruitful sacrifices
Offered to Thee in a column of smoke,
Inhale these offerings of mine.
Accept in kindness, not in wrath
The bouquet of my little words
—The voluntary gift of my sacrifice—
It is offered up to Thee
As if forced by the fattened sins of my soul.
Permit these, my secret yearnings,
To rise up without delay to Thee—
These feelings from the depths of my heart.

A word with God . . . . Naregatsi composed ninety-five of these prayers, each beginning with this invocation. This is an abridged version of the first prayer, omitting the final ten lines. See Torkom Patriarch Koushagian, *Nareg Prayer Book, Krikor Naregatsi* (Cairo, Egypt: H. Azablar, 1926), pp. 1-2, for a modern Armenian translation.

Ներսէս Շնորհալի
Nerses Shnorali
1102–1173

Չարթի՛ք

Չարթի՛ք, փրկեալք արեամբ,
Եւ տուք զփառն փրկողին, ալէլուիա:
    Չարթի՛ք, նոր ժողովուրդք,
    Նոր երգս առեալ նորոգողին, ալէլուիա:
Չարթի՛ք, Հարսունք Հոգւով՝
Սպասեալ գալոյ սուրբ փեսային, ալէլուիա:
    Չարթի՛ք, վառեալք լուսով՝
    Ըստ իմաստուն սուրբ կուսանացն, ալէլուիա:
Չարթի՛ք, պատրաստեցէք իւղ լապտերաց,
գՁերմ արտասուս, ալէլուիա:
    Չարթի՛ք եւ մի ննջէք՝
    Նման յիմար կուսից նիրհէք, ալէլուիա:
Չարթի՛ք, երկիր պագցրւք,
Եւ արտասուօք զայս ասացուք, ալէլուիա:

Awake

Awake, you who are saved by His blood,
Glorify the Savior, halleluia.
    Awake, all you new nations,
    Sing songs to the Redeemer, halleluia.
Wake up your souls all you maidens,
Come, attend the holy Groom, halleluia.
    Wake you wise virgins, as is your custom,
    Be bright with hope, halleluia.
Wake, prepare oil for the lanterns,
And weep warm tears, halleluia.
    Wake, and do not fall asleep
    As foolish virgins do, halleluia.
Wake all and be worshipful
And weep, singing halleluia.

Ֆրիկ

Frig

thirteenth–fourteenth centuries

Բան ի Ֆրիկ Գրքոյն

Աստուած արդար ես յիրալի,
Եւ ողորմած յամենայնի.
Հանդէս ունիմ բան մի վիճի,
Թէ դու լսես քո ծառայի։

Այս է գարմանք հիանալի,
Որ կու լինի վերայ երկրի.
Եւ հիացումն ազգի ազգի,
զՈր տեսանեմք ի յաշխարհի։

Գէմ մէկ Ադամ էր ի դրախտին,
Եւ մէկն Եւայ իւր նմանին.
Եւ մէկ բարբառ համազգային,
Մինչեւ կերեալ պտղոյ ծառին։

Արդ այս բանս է հիանալի,
Եւ առաւել գարմանալի.
Թէ մէկ Ադամ եւ յԵւայէ
Ո՞րքան ազգեր ծնան յերկրի։

Որ մէկն ապրի տասն տարի,
Մէկն հարիւր այլ աւելի.
Մէկն ո՛չ ի տան հասանի,
Երկու երեք ամսոց մեռնի։

Մէկն ի պապանց պարոնորդի,
Մէկն ի հարանց մուրող լինի.
Մէկին հազար ձի եւ ջորի,
Մէկին ո՛չ ուլ մի, ոչ մաքի։

Մէկին ատլաս եւ դրմգի,
Մէկին շապիկ մի չի հասնի.
Մէկին հարամն յաջողի,
Մէկին հալալն կորուսի։

Մէկն նման է Ցուդայի,
Սպանող, դամազ, գործող չարի.
Տեղի եղեալ սատանայի
Եւ բնակարան դիւաց դասի։

Ֆրիկ / 50

Complaint

O just and righteous God,
You who have mercy on us all,
I have a bone to pick with You
If You will only listen to Your servant's plaint.

It is really quite astonishing
To observe what takes place on earth,
So many wonders in many forms
We see in this, our world.

Wasn't there only one Adam in heaven,
And only one Eve from his side,
And only a single language for all
Before the fruit from the tree was eaten?

Now this particular thing is amazing,
And, even more, bewildering:
From only one Adam and only one Eve
So many nations came forth.

One man lives for ten years,
Another a hundred or more,
Another doesn't even reach ten years
But dies in two months or three.

One is descended from a wealthy lord,
Another, on his father's side, a bum;
One owns a thousand mules and horses,
Another owns neither goat nor kid.

One wears glossy purple cloth,
Another lacks even a shirt;
One grows rich by foul dealings,
Another fails although his cause is just.

One is a Judas Iscariot—
A murderer and cruel in his heart,
His place is the home of the devil,
A house for Satan's band.

Ես քեզ մեղայ երկնաւորի,
Տեառն Աստուծոյ ահեղ մեծի․
Քո դատաստանն է յիրաւի,
Նեաթով կուլ տաս ամէն մէկի։

Տէ՛ր, քո կամացն է աշխարհա լի,
Այսպէս լինել զոր ասացի․
Քեզ օրհնութիւն ի մէնջ տացի,
Ամենազօր Տեառնդ Յիսուսի։

I, a poor mortal, beg your pardon,
O great, all-transcendent Lord,
Your judgments are just and righteous,
Your decrees given with an even hand.

Lord, the world is full of Your will,
Things are much as I have said:
Blessings from all of us on You,
On Lord Jesus, Your almighty son.

Կոստանդին Երզնկացի
Konstantin Yerzengatsi
thirteenth–fourteenth centuries

Տաղ Սիրոյ

Հանց գեղեցիկ մօրմ ու շիտակ,
Պատկեր գեղով առ յիս հասաւ,
Այլ չէ՛ տեսեր մարդ կենդանի
զԱյն, որ իմ աչքս տեսաւ։

զՕրն ես ի իւր սէրն կենամ,
Ցերագ հետ իւր տեսուն գնամ,
զԱշքերս արեամբ հետ իւր թանամ՝
Ջերայ հոգիս յինէն տարաւ։

Երբ որ անուշ հոտն յիս բուրեց՝
Զիս ի խելաց շուտով թափեց։
Ի յայն պահուն սիրոս իմ եփեց՝
Երբ իւր տեսն ինձ երեւեցաւ։

Ջերդ գլուսին սուրաթ բոլոր,
Շուրջ գերեսին մազերն ոլոր,
Անով արեր է շատ մոլոր՝
Ընցտի լուսով յիս ցաթեցաւ։

Թէ սիրտ ունիմ՝ սէր անվճար,
Որ բամնելոյ այլ չկայ ճար,
Նա իմ հոգոյս եղեր տաճար,
Իմ աչերուս լոյս ծագեցաւ։

Ակն գոհար է յիր շարած,
Ներքեւ շրթանցն պատրաստած,
Տեսն իւր կարմիր է զարդարած՝
զԻնչ բուրաստանք, որ ծաղկեցաւ։

զԻնչ որ հագնի, նա իւր վայլէ.
Երբ գունգգուն ելնէ՝ փայլէ,
զերկիր ի իւր լուսոյն հալէ,
Հանց՝ որ չաստոց սիրտ մաշեցաւ։

Ես իմ կարօտ ի իւր սիրուն՝
զԻնչ ճարաւած երկիր ցօղոյն,
Կամ զինչ գարնան անուշ քամուն՝
Թէ ե՛րբ հնչէ հողմըն հարաւ։

Love Song

So beautiful, tender, so gentle,
So stunning a maiden came my way,
That save for these eyes of mine
No living soul has seen her like.

By day I hold to her love inside me,
And go to see her often;
Since the day she drained my soul from me
My reddened eyes drip tears upon her face.

When her soft fragrance filled the air
Straightaway I felt my senses vanish;
From the time that I first glimpsed her,
My heart has been on fire.

O she has a face, round as the moon,
Her curly hair floats around her head,
O her beauty leaves many a man enchanted:
It seems as if brilliant light now falls on me.

In my heart flames an undying love
That nothing here can ever quench,
She has become a temple in my soul—
And a strong light now shines from my eyes.

Set behind her lips are rows
Of gems and precious stones;
Fragrant, clothed in purple, her figure
Is a garden of sweet-scented flowers.

All that she wears becomes her;
When she rises, walks lightly away,
The world melts from all her brilliance,
And the hearts of many men lie crumbled.

I long for her love
As the thirsting land longs for dew,
Or for the sweet cool spring breeze
When the hot southern wind blows.

Քանի որ լիմ տեսուս պատեր՝
Կենաց ճարակն է ինձ հատեր,
Լացն ու հառաչն է դիս պատեր,
Հոգու քաղիլ ու սրտացալ։

Զնա երբ ի խաղ տեսնում նագով,
Լուսին սուրբաթ, սխահ մագով,
Ես իւր դէմն ելնեմ սագով
Եւ թէ ծառայ լինիմ կամով։

Յայնժամ լինի այն մեզ նշան,
Որժամ խմեմ գլի շիշան
Նռան գունով գգինին ռաւշան՝
Որ քո տեսուղ նմանեցաւ։

Քանի° խոսիս բանք ի ժողով
Է՛ Կոստանդի՛ն, բարձր պոյով,
Կամ անցաւոր բանք սխալով
Ընդէ°ր ի քէն հանց գովեցաւ։

Եղբարք մի կան հետ մեզ սիրով,
Աշխարհի բան ուզեն գրով․
Նա ես վասն այն յայտնի ճայնով
Սիրու բաներս ասցի յօլով։

*

Դարձիր յունայն սուտ բաներուտ,
Չի է անչած եւ անօգուտ,
Խելոք իմաստութիւնդ մուտ
Չի քեզ բաժին իրք մ'այլ անկաւ։

The moment she passes from my view,
My reason for living is gone:
I am walled in by tears and sighs,
My heart aches and my spirit is faint.

When I see her, raven-haired, dancing demurely,
The very image of the moon itself,
I fall before her with my saz
And freely become her servant.

And only then shall I know bliss,
When I can drain the brimming cup
Filled with the pomegranate's bright wine—
Whose color is most like her face.

All the things you say when meeting friends,
O tall, shapely Konstantin,
Things that pass, fleeting, errant thoughts—
Why do you think them worth praise?

There are brothers, ever loving brothers,
Who want great songs of the soil composed;
But behold, in a quavering voice
I am endlessly singing lovesongs.

*

Turn away from false, vain things,
They serve no use or profit,
Judge with reason and wisdom,
For there will be yet another affair.

Saz, stringed instrument used by troubadours.

Գրիգորիս Աղթամարցի
Grigoris Akhtamartsi
fifteenth–sixteenth centuries

Տաղ ի Վերայ Նորաշէն Տուն եւ Այգի
Ունեցողի եւ Լալու

Յամէն առաւօտ եւ լոյս
Գաբրիէլն ասէր հոգոյս.
«Արի՛, ե՛լ ի յայս այգոյս»,
Այս իմ նորատունկ այգոյս։

Քար եմ բերեր սարերոյս,
Փուշ եմ կրեր ձորերոյս,
Պատ եմ բոլորեր այգոյս,
Կ՚ասեն, թ՚«Արե՛կ, ե՛լ այգոյս»։

Ինչպէ՞ս ելնեմ ի յայգոյս,
Գէմ չար փուշ կայ պատերոյս։

Ջուր եմ բերեր լեռներոյս,
Ադրիւր եմ շիներ այգոյս,
Դեռ չեմ խմեր ի ջրոյս,
Կ՚ասեն, թ՚«Արե՛կ, ե՛լ այգոյս»։

Ուռ եմ տնկեր այս այգոյս,
գՃակն եմ ջրեր այս տնկոյս,
Դեռ չեմ կերեր ի պտղոյս,
Կ՚ասեն, թէ՛ «Արե՛կ, ե՛լ այգոյս»...

Հնձան եմ շիներ այգոյս,
Կարաս եմ թաղեր գինոյս,
Դեռ չեմ խմեր ի գինոյս,
Կ՚ասեն, թ՚«Արե՛կ, ե՛լ այգոյս»։
Այս իմ նորաշէն տներոյս։

Տուն եմ շիներ մէջ այգոյս,
Ոսկով նաշխած չարօրբխուս,
Դեռ չեմ վայլեր չէնքերոյս,
Կ՚ասեն, թ՚«Արե՛կ, ե՛լ այգոյս»...

Վարդ եմ տնկեր այս այգոյս,
Կարմիր 'ւ րապիտակ վարդոյս,
Դեռ չեմ գՀոտն առեր գվարդոյս,
Կ՚ասեն, թ՚«Արե՛կ, ե՛լ այգոյս»։

Song to Weeping, and to the Owner of a New-built House and Garden

Every morning at daybreak
Gabriel tells my soul
"Come, get away from my garden."
—This, my freshly sown garden.

I bore rocks from the mountains,
And brought thistles from the valley,
Built a wall round my garden
—I'm told, "Come, get away from my garden."

How shall I leave my garden?
There are so many thorns on the walls.

I carried water from the mountains,
In my garden I let in a spring;
I have not yet drunk from the spring
—I'm told, "Come, get away from my garden."

I planted vines in the garden,
And I watered them deep;
I have yet to taste of their fruit
—I'm told, "Come, get away from my garden."

In my garden I built a threshing floor,
I laid in a jar for the wine;
I have yet to drink from the wine
—I'm told, "Come, get away from my garden,
—Out of my new-built house!"

I built a house in my garden,
And covered the rooms with gilt;
I have yet to enjoy my house
—I'm told, "Come, get away from my house."

I planted roses in my garden,
Fragrant white and red roses;
I have yet to smell my roses
—I'm told, "Come, get away from my garden."

Ծադիկ եմ տնկեր այդոյս,
Կանաչ ուլ դեդին ծադկոյս,
Դեռ չեմ գհոտն առեր ծադկոյս,
Կ'ասեն, թ' «Աբ'եկ, ե'լ այդոյս»...

Գաբբիէլն եկաւ հոգոյս,
Յահէն կապեցաւ լեզուս,
Խաւբաւ աչերս ի լալոյս,
Աւա'ղ իմ կաբձ աբեւուս,
Կ'ասեն, թ' «Աբ'եկ, ե'լ այդոյս»։

Առին գհոգիս ի մաբմնոյս,
Հանեցին գիս յիմ այդոյս,
Մահ է, որ ելնեմ այդոյս,
Այս իմ նոբաշէն տներոյս։

Ուռն կանաչ է այդոյս,
Որթն բացեալ է տնկոյս,
Խաղողն գոյնգդոյն այդոյս,
Ծառեր-տունկն շատ՝ այդոյս,
Կ'ասեն, թ' «Աբ'եկ, ե'լ այդոյս»։

Պուլպուլն կանչէ այդոյս
Առաւօտէն մինչ ի լոյս,
Յօղն իջանէ ի յայդոյս
յԱմէն առաւօտ եւ լոյս։

I planted flowers in my garden,
My flowers grow green and golden;
I have yet to smell my flowers
—I'm told, "Come, get away from my garden."

Gabriel came to take my soul,
Frightened, I could not speak;
Tears welled and dimmed my eyes
(O the short-lived term of my sun)
—I'm told, "Come, get away from my garden."

They stripped my body from my soul,
They cast me out of my garden—
It is death to be gone from my garden,
To be gone from my new-built house.

The vines are green in my garden,
They have put forth many tendrils,
And the grapes are of many hues,
My garden is filled with trees and shrubs
—I'm told, "Come, get away from my garden."

The nightingale calls from my garden,
From dawn to sunrise it calls,
And every morning at daybreak
The dew settles down on my garden.

Յովհաննէս Թլկուրանցի
Hovhanness Telkurantsi
fifteenth–sixteenth centuries

Տաղ Սիրոյ

Ցանկարծակի մէկ մի տեսայ, որ կու ցօղայ դոյն երեսէն,
Թալցայ, անկեայ ի տեսիլենէն, չողայր կաթէր լոյան ի վզէն։
Աչքերն է ծով, ունքն է թուխ ամպ, մազն է դեղձան ոսկի թելէն,
Զինքն ճօճար՝ դէտ գուրի ճեղ, Հրով այրէր զերկիր ամէն։
Ծռխագնաց մանրաքայլող, հոգիքն ի մարմնէ քակող,
Լութֆն է ծագեր զամէն աշխարհս, շաքար կաթէր իւր քարամէն։
Երբ իմ աչերս ի քեզ դիպաւ, նայ վառեցաւ դէտ մոմեղէն։
Խելագնաց ի վայր մնացի, գարհուրեցայ ի տեսիլենէն։
Խեւ Յովհաննէս Թլկուրանցի, խիստ մի հաներ գոռք է ծրէն,
Աղէկ սուրաթ երբ մեռանի, ցամքի, զնայ դոյն երեսէն։

Song of Love

Suddenly I saw a face, radiant with color.
I grew faint when I saw the shimmering light of her neck.
Her eyes are seas, her brows thick clouds, her hair is woven gold.

She sways like a willow branch, and sets the world on fire.
Her delicate footfalls distinguish her soul from her body,
Grace spreads over the earth, and honey scents the air around her.

When I caught sight of her, I flamed, I burned,
I was so overcome, I lost my senses.
"Foolish Hovhanness Telkurantsi, really! Don't place your foot beyond the ledge:
When a once radiant face has withered, the color fades from it, before it dies."

Նահապետ Քուչակ
Nahabed Kouchag
sixteenth century

Խոհեր

—Ես՝ աչք ու դու՝ լույս, Հոգի՛, առանց լույս՝ աչքն խավարի,
Ես՝ ձուկ ու դու՝ ջուր, Հոգի՛, առանց ջուր՝ ձուկն մեռանի.
Երբ գձուկն ի ջրէն հանեն 'լ ի այլ ջուր ձգեն, նա ապրի,
Երբ զիս ի քենէ զատեն, քան զմեռնելն այլ ճար չի լինի։

« »

—Քանի՛ ու քանի՛ ասեմ, վարդն մի՛ սիրեր, փուշ ունի.
Գնա՛ մանուշակ սիրէ, փուշ չունի, անուշ հոտ ունի.
Վարդն բացուած մի՛ սիրեր, որ գայ ի ծոցդ թառամի.
Վարդն պլպլուլիկ սիրէ, որ գայ ի ծոցդ ուբացուլի։

« »

Ես այն հալերուն էի, որ գետինն կուտ չլուտէի.
Թուչ'ի երկնոքն երթ՛ի, թէ սիրոյ ակնատն չընկնէի.
Ակնատն ի ծովուն միջին էր լարած 'լ ես չգիտէի.
Ամէն հալ ուռոքն ընկնէր, ես ուռօքս ութելս ալելի։

« »

Եկին ուխապար բերին, թէ քո եարն եղեր հաբեղայ.
Փուշ արմացքն գիս պատեց, թէ նա ո՞նց եղալ հաբեղայ.
Բերնիկն էր շաքրի սովոր, աճապ ո՞նց կերալ նա բակլայ.
Անձիկն էր շապկի սովոր, աճապ ո՞նց հագաւ ան վալայ։

« »

Քանի մարն գիս բերեր, քահանի չեմ խոստովաներ.
Ուրտեղ քահանայ տեսեր, նա ծռեր ճամբուս ու ելեր.
Ուրտեղ մէկ ադուոր տեսեր, գիրկ ու ծող 'լ ի դէմ գնացեր.
Մոցիկն եմ ժամուն արել, ծծերուն եմ խոստովաներ։

« »

Thoughts

I am the eye and you the light, my soul, without light the eye is dark.
I am like the fish and you the water, my soul, without water the fish
is dead.
When the fish is removed from water but returned to it, it can live,
But when they take me from you I'll die, and there'll be no remedy.

<< >>

How often have I said don't love the rose, it carries thorns;
Go love the violet, it has no thorns and offers a gentle scent.
Don't love the blossomed rose, lest it wither on your breast,
Love only the budding rose, that it may come to your heart and
bloom there.

<< >>

I was one of the birds who didn't seek for grain on the ground,
I would always fly, fly and avoid the snare of love.
But my snare had been set in the sea, though about that I knew
nothing;
Every bird stood trapped by its feet, but I stood trapped, both feet
and arms.

<< >>

The news was brought that my beloved had become a nun;
I was completely astonished, I wondered how such a thing could be—
A mouth used only to sweets must now chew only coarse grains.
A body used only to silks must now suffer in dull, rough cloth.

<< >>

Since I was born of a woman, I will not confess to a priest,
Wherever I've seen a priest, I've changed my path and gone off;
Wherever I've caught sight of a beauty, I've approached her with
open arms and heart,
I've made a chapel of her heart, made my confession only on her
breasts.

<< >>

—Քո ծոցդ է ճերմակ տաճար, քո ծծերդ է կանթեդ ի վառ.
Երթամ ես ժամկոչ ըլլամ, գամ լինիմ տաճրիդ լուսարար։
—Գնա՛, ծո տղա՛յ տխմար, չի վայլես տաճրիս լուսարար,
Երթաս դուն խաղով լինաս ու թողուս տաճարս ի խալար։

«   »

—Իմ բարձրագնայ լուսին, յո՞ւր կ'երթաս գիշերդ անհուն.
Շատ յերդիք ի վար հային, կու տեսնես շատ կիլզել ի քուն.
զԿոճկին ալ արձակ արբեր, լոյս դիպեր ի մէջ ծծերուն.
Շառափիդ յերկինս տուեր, խալաբեր լոյան աստղերուն։

«   »

—Լուսին, պարծենաս, ասես. «Լուս կու տամ ես աստըներորիս»։
Աճա Հողեղէն լուսին ի գրկիս ՚ւ երեսն երեսիս.
Թէ չես աւտալ այս գերուն, յետ տանեմ զփէշ կապայիս,
Վախեմ՝ սիրոյ տէր լինիս, լուս պակաս տաս աստըներորիս։

«   »

—Սուտ է, որ կ'ասեն, եղբարք, թ՚ ընտանի կաքաւ չի լինի.
Մէկիկ մ՚ես երէկ տեսայ, ՚ւ երնեկ է գիր տեռն որ ունի.
Ունեըն էր դալամով քաշած, ՚ւ իր բեռանն շաքրով ի լի.
զՄեռելն այլ ի գիրկն առնուր, ի ծոցուն հանէր կենդանի։

«   »

Ես՝ տղայ ու դուն՝ տղայ, սիրելուն ատենն է հիմա.
Մէջկունքդ աղեղան նման, քանի ես քաջեմ, նա կու գայ.
Քո ճիճղ է խաղող նման ու առեր կբծցցդ ի վերայ.
Քո ծոցդ առաւօտ նման, քանի յետ բանամ, նա լուսնայ։

«   »

Գիշերն ես ի քուն էի, իմ սրտիս ականջն էր ի բաց.
Սիրու հաւն ի ճայն եած, լոք լսեց սրտիկս ու դողաց.
Կու թուէր իմ եարին լեզուն ան հալուն բեռանն էր դրած.
Ո՛վ իմ սրտիս գանգտին ան հալուն էր հասկըցուցած։

«   »

Your heart is my white temple, and your breasts are holy lanterns,
I will be your sexton, a sacristan who guards the shrine.
O go, stupid boy, you're unworthy to be sexton of this temple,
Go play, let my temple smoulder in the dark.

<< >>

O my high, roaming moon, where do you go through the broad night?
You peer through the rooftops and see the girls asleep—
They have loosened their clothes, and your brightness across their
                                                                               breasts
Makes a brilliance that pales the stars.

<< >>

Moon, you boast and say, "I bring light to a dark world."
But here I hold the earthly moon, her face warm against mine.
And should you not believe a slave like me, I'd pull the blanket down—
Except I'm afraid you too would tumble into love, and so shed less
                                                    light upon the world.

<< >>

Brothers, they lie when they say you cannot tame a peacock—
I saw one only the other day, whose owner I truly envy:
Her eyebrows were drawn with pencil and her mouth was sweet
                                                                    as honey,
She could press a dead man to her, then let him go—alive.

<< >>

I am young and so are you, and now is the time for love.
Your waist is like a bow: as I draw, it comes closer.
Like mounds of grapes are your breasts, set full on your bosom,
Your breasts are like the morning: the more they are revealed,
                                the more brilliant they look.

<< >>

During the night I slept, but my heart stayed awake,
It heard love singing like a bird, and my heart started trembling
                                                                  to hear it;
Love was singing with my dear one's voice, singing with the voice
                                                                 of a bird—
Who could have shown my heart's complaint to love?

<< >>

—Ա՛յ իմ փոքրիկ շամամ, քո ծոցուղ, ա՛մ, է°րբ տիրանամ.
Քո ծոցդ է ի ծով նման, ծովն դեզ կ'ասեն ի ջերման.
Փոքրիկ մրտեմնիկ լինամ ու մտնամ ի ծոցդ ու լողամ.
Մովուղ ալ ի դուրս ելնամ, ունեբուղ շուքն քնանամ։

« »

Այս ծովական գիշերս ի քուն՝ ես երկու շրջան մանեցի.
Խոշ եարս ալ ի միտս ընկաւ, թեգ մ'ելյայ գշահրաս վերուցի,
Փարչիկ մ'այլ գինի առի, խոշ եարիս դուռն դնացի.
—Խոշ եար, ա'մ, զդուռն բաց, ճիւն եկեր, ուփիս կու մսի։

« »

—Ա՛յ իմ նշենի ծաղիկ, ծաղկեցար ու դարձար ի նուշ.
Բերանդ է աղուշ-մաղուշ, պղկըներդ է արմաւ ու նուշ.
Ջայախդ որ սփիղ ունիս, դու խմէ, որ ասեմ՝ Անո՛ւշ.
Պաղեմ գայդ բերնիղ բոլորն, որ գինուլն Հոտն գայ անուշ։

« »

—Այս ծովական գիշերս ես ի դուրող անկաջ աւարա.
Կա'մ առ գիս ի ծոցդ ի քուն, կա'մ տեստուբ արա, թէ՝ գնա՛.
    —Ինչպէ°ս ասեմ, թէ՝ գնա՛, — մանկան սիրան չիսմէ կու մնայ.
Աբ'եկ, որ զքեզ ծոցս առնեմ, տեզ շինեմ կրծոցս ի վերայ,
Մոցս քեզ սեղան շինեմ, ճիծա բարձ՝ երեսդ ի վերայ։
Կոճիկա կոճեմ վերայ, որ շնչիկդ ի ծոցս ելնայ։

O my little one, shall I ever conquer your bosom?
Your breast is like a sea, a sea cool to my fever,
Let me be like a little salamander, who enters the sea of your breast
                                    and swims there,
Then gets away only to rest in the shade cast by your lashes.

<< >>

This whole cold night through till dawn I sat spinning two rows
                                    of yarn,
My delightful love came to mind and quickly I quit my work;
I took a small pitcher filled with wine, and went to the door of my love:
"Quick, open the door my sweet one, there is snow on the ground and
                                      my feet are cold."

<< >>

O my almond blossom, you bloomed and became delicious,
Your mouth is honey sweet, your lips rich as almond and dates,
Drink from the cup of wine you hold, that I may say sweet touches
                                        sweet.
O I shall kiss all around your mouth, whence comes the fragrance of
                                        wine.

<< >>

On this cold night, forsaking my work, I come to your door,
Either let me sleep upon your breast, or tell me to go.
    How can I say 'Go,' will not your gentle heart be cross with me?
    Come, let me take you to my heart, make a place for you on my
                                        breast,
        Mold my bosom into an altar, make my breasts a pillow so your face
                                        can lie full upon them,
            Fasten my cape and hold you in so that your breath will always be
                                        warm upon my breast.

Ներսէս Մոկացի
Nerses Mokatsi
seventeenth century

Վիճաբանութիւն երկնի եւ երկրի

Երկինքն ու գետինքն եղբարք,
Ածապ ո՞ր քան գործն ալելի.—
զերկնից բարձրութիւն ասեմ,
Նա գետնին պտուղն ալելի։

Երկինք գետնին ասաց.
—Բան ունեմ քանց քեզ ալելի.
զՊայծառագուն աստղունքս,
Ամէնն իմ կողմէս կու լինի։

Գետինն երկրնուցն ասաց.
—Աստուծոյ մունաթն ալելի.
Վեցհազարագուն ծաղկունքս,
Ամէն իմ կողմէս կու լինի։

Երկինքն գետնին ասաց.
—Բան ունիմ քանց քեզ ալելի.
Իմ ցողն ի քենէ կտրեմ.
Քո ծաղկունքն որո՞վ գարդարի։

Գետինն երկրնուցն ասաց.
—Աստուծոյ մունաթն ալելի.
Դու ցողն ի ծովուն կ'առնես,
Ծովուն ակն յիանէ կու լինի.
զԻմ ակն որ ի յիս քաշեմ՝
Նա քո ցողն ուստի՞ց կու լինի։

Երկինքն գետնին ասաց.
—Բան ունիմ քանց քեզ ալելի.
Պարգեմ, բարկ արեւ դիպեմ,
Քո ծաղկունքն ամէնըն խշրի։

Գետինն երկրնուցն ասաց.
—Աստուծոյ մունաթն ալելի.
Ջուրն ի յանդնդոցն հանեմ,
Որ ծաղկունքն ամէն գարդարի։

Երկինքն գետնին ասաց.
—Բան ունիմ քանց քեզ ալելի.
Կայծակ ու կարկուտ անեմ,
Քո ծաղկունքն ամէն խափանի։

Argument between the Sky and Earth

The sky and the earth are brothers,
I wonder which is stronger?
Shall I measure the height of the sky,
Shall I count the fruits of the earth?

The sky said to the earth:
"I have something more than you—
These brightly shimmering stars
All issue from me."

The earth said to the sky:
"God's grace to me is greater—
Six-thousand colorful flowers
All issue from me."

The sky said to the earth:
"I have something more than you—
If I should cut short the dew,
How could your flowers bloom?"

The earth said to the sky:
"God's grace to me is greater—
Though you capture the dew from the sea,
I am the source of the sea;
If I should dry up the sea,
Where will you get the dew?"

The sky said to the earth:
"I have something more than you—
If on a cloudless day I set the sun
To burn, your flowers will all be seared."

The earth said to the sky:
"God's grace to me is greater—
I'll draw up water from the depths
So the flowers may bloom again."

The sky said to the earth:
"I have something more than you—
Should I bring down hail and lightning,
All your flowers, all will wash away."

Mokatsi

Գետինն երկրնուցն ասաց.
—Աստուծոյ մուննաթն աւելի.
Անչափ սար ու ձոր ունիմ
Քո կարկուտն ի մէջն կը լցուի:

Երկինքն գետնին ասաց.
—Բան ունիմ քանց քեզ աւելի.
Ուր ադէկ կորին մ'որ կայ
Գայ ի քո ներքեւ զըստանի:

Գետինն երկրնուցն ասաց.
—Աստուծոյ մուննաթն աւելի.
Աստուած իր տուած հոգին
Թէ կ'առնէ՝ նա ի՞նչ տի լինի:

Թէ մարմին ի յիս չառնեմ,
Նա աշխարհ հոտուն անցանի,
Հրեշտակք հոտուն փախչեն,
Երկինք ու գետինք տատանի:

Երկինքն գետնին ասաց.
—Բան ունիմ քանց քեզ աւելի.
Ինն դասք Հրեշտակք որ կան
Ամէնն իմ կողմէս կու լինին:

Գետինն երկրնուցն ասաց.
—Աստուծոյ մուննաթն աւելի.
Սուրբ առաքեալք, մարգարէք
Ամէնն իմ կողմէս կու լինին:

Երկինքն գետնին ասաց.
—Բան ունիմ քանց քեզ աւելի.
Եօթն տակ երկինքն եմ ես,
Ուր արեւ, լուսին կու լինի.
Ստեղծողն Արարիչն Աստուած
Աթոռով վրաս կը բազմի:

Գետինն երկրնուցն ասաց.
—Աստուծոյ մուննաթն աւելի.
Եօթն տակ երկինքդ ասեմ,
Այն ամէնն ի վայր թափի.
Արեւ ու լուսին, աստղունքն
Որ երթան ի հետ խաղարին,
Եւ քո Արարիչն Աստուած

The earth said to the sky:
"God's grace to me is greater—
I have so many hills and dales,
That all your hail will gather there."

The sky said to the earth:
"I have something more than you—
Wherever there's a good stalwart man
He lies with others in your charnel house."

The earth said to the sky:
"God's grace to me is greater—
God takes back the souls He gives,
What is so mournful in that?

Should I not take in the bodies,
Their smell would spread over the world;
Angels would fly from the smell,
And earth and sky get mixed together."

The sky said to the earth:
"I have something more than you:
Nine groups of angels live with me,
And all have their birthplace in me."

The earth said to the sky:
"God's grace to me is greater—
The holy disciples, the prophets,
All have their birthplace in me."

The sky said to the earth:
"I have something more than you—
The seven levels of heaven are mine,
Where the sun and moon live—
The Creator, Almighty God,
Sits enthroned with me."

The earth said to the sky:
"God's grace to me is greater—
Your seven levels of heaven,
All of them will topple down;
The sun and the moon and the stars
Will also follow the dark,
And God, your Creator,

Աթոռով ի վայր տի իջնի,
Դատաստան դետին տի լինի։

Ահա ցածացաւ երկինքն
Ու դգլուխ եղիր դետանի...
Դուք այլ ցնծացէ՛ք, մանկտիք,
Գլուխ դրէք դետօրնի,
Քան դերկին ի՞նչ բարձր կայ,
Որ գլուխ եդեր դետօրնի։
Այսօր վերան կու քայլենք,
Վաղն տի մտնունք ներքեւ հողի։

Will descend from His throne
And make his Last Judgment."

Here the sky came lower,
Laid its head on the earth—
"You, too, O children, rejoice
And bow your heads on the earth.
What is there above the sky
That also bows down to earth?
Today we will walk upon it,
Tomorrow we will enter it."

Նաղաշ Յովնաթան
Nagash Hovnaton
seventeenth–eighteenth centuries

Տաղ Սիրոյ

Ե՛կ, դնամք պաղշէն, նստեմք բոլորն շարած վարդի․—
Ամա՛ն, ամա՛ն, քո սիրոյդ եղեր եմ տալու տիվանայ․—
Ճոցիդ եմիշներն ինճնէ պատ նշանց չտա՛ս ուրիշ մարդի․—
Ամա՛ն, ամա՛ն, քո սիրոյդ եղեր եմ տալու տիվանայ։

Խալերդ պայծառ աստղունք, երեսդ է բոլոր լուսին,
Սիաճ ծամերդ ընկած քո թիկունքին եւ ուսին.
Քո գարդէն ես կու մեանիմ, ինչ լայեզ է քո նամուսին.
Ամա՛ն, ամա՛ն քո սիրոյդ եղեր եմ տալու տիվանայ։

Լեզուդ քաղցրախոս բլբուլ, ատամներդ մարգարտաշար,
Ճոցդ բաղչայ, կանանչ բոստան, չամամ, խնձոր շարեջար․
Ընկայ քո մեղաց ծովըն, էլ չի մնաց հոգւոյ պաչար.
Ամա՛ն, ամա՛ն քո սիրոյդ եղեր եմ տալու տիվանայ։

Ունքերդ կապած կամար՝ թրի նման կու շողշողայ․
Աչքերդ եաղի ջալլադ, որ տեսնեմ, սիրտս կու դողայ,
Երանի տամ այն մարդին, որ քու ծոցումդ կու լողայ.
Ամա՛ն, ամա՛ն, քո սիրոյդ եղեր եմ տալու տիվանայ։

Աստուա՛ծ սիրէք, դնացէ՛ք, տեսէ՛ք թէ իմ եարըն տա՞նն ա․
Երթա՛մ, աղաչե՛մ, բալքի լռաճմ անի, դուռըն բանայ,
Մէկ բերան ինձ խօսի, որ էրած սիրտս հովանայ․
Ամա՛ն, ամա՛ն, քո սիրոյդ եղեր եմ տալու տիվանայ։

Առաւօտուց կարմիր ցօղըն կարմիր վարդին վրայ մաղած,
Իմ սիրելին ինձ համար տե՞ս, քանի ցեզ վարդ է քաղած․—
Նորա սիրոյ կրակովըն իմ սրտին մէջըն է տաղած։
Ամա՛ն, ամա՛ն, քո սիրոյդ եղեր եմ տալու տիվանայ։

Սիրամարգի նման ես, դատ ու գարբափով գարդարած,
Մէկ համբուրելոյ համար ես մնացել եմ պաչարած,
Նաղաշըն է՞ր կը սպանես, տեսնեմ, թէ քեզ ի՞նչ եմ արած․
Ամա՛ն, ամա՛ն, քո սիրոյդ եղեր եմ տալու տիվանայ։

Song of Love

Come, let's go into the garden and sit among the roses.
O dear, O dear, my love of you has made me truly mad;
Don't display your ripe breasts to anyone but me—
O dear, O dear, my love of you has made me truly mad.

Your skin is bright as stars, your face a rounded moon,
Your black hair falls softly down your neck and shoulders;
I'll die from worry over you—how that will suit your pride!
O dear, O dear, my love of you has made me truly mad.

Your voice is sweet as a nightingale's, your teeth are rows of pearls,
Your breast's a meadow, lush garden, round fruit, bright apples;
Into the sea of your sins I fell: most of my soul is drowned.
O dear, O dear, my love of you has made me truly mad.

Your gleaming brows curve finely as a sword,
Your defiant eyes make my heart tremble when I catch them;
And he will be blissful, who lives in your heart.
O dear, O dear, my love of you has made me truly mad.

For God's sake, go and see if my love is home;
Let me go, let me plead, she may pity me and open the door,
Should she speak to me but once, I know her quivering heart will
                              start to cool.
O dear, O dear, my love of you has made me truly mad.

Since morning, the dew shines red on these red roses;
See the many kinds of roses my love has picked for me?
The fire of my love for her has seared my heart.
O dear, O dear, my love of you has made me truly mad.

Dressed in bright colors and adorned with gold, you are splendid as a
                              peacock;
Seeking for a single kiss, I run around bewildered.
Is it Nagash you would kill? What have I ever done to you?
O dear, O dear, my love of you has made me truly mad.

Բաղդասար Դպիր
Psalm-reader (Tbir) Baghdassar
eighteenth century

Տաղ

Ի ննջմանէդ արքայական,
Զարթի՛ր, նազելի իմ, զարթի՛ր,
Եհաս նշոյլն արեգական,—
Զարթի՛ր, նազելի իմ, զարթի՛ր:

Պատկեր սիրուն, տիպ բոլորակ,
Լրացելոյ լուսնոյն քաատակ,
Ո՛չ գտանի քեզ օրինակ,—
Զարթի՛ր, նազելի իմ, զարթի՛ր:

Այդ քո տեսիլդ, գոր դու ունիս,
Արաբ ծառայ քեզ զգերիս,
Արեւակէզ գուցէ լինիս,—
Զարթի՛ր, նազելի իմ, զարթի՛ր:

Ղաբին սրտիւ, քանի՞ կոծամ,
Է՛ վարդ կարմիր եւ անթառամ,
Տե՛ս, թէ զիա՞րդ խղճալի կամ,—
Զարթի՛ր, նազելի իմ, զարթի՛ր:

Տապ եւ խորշակ ժամանեցին,
զԹերթիկ գեղոյդ այրել կամին,
Փանգի չանց գիշերն մթին,
Զարթի՛ր, նազելի իմ, զարթի՛ր:

Է՛ աննմանն իմ գովելիս,
Ի մէջ ականց գեղ քո՝ մագնիս,
Ի ռահեակ սոյն թուականիս,
Զարթի՛ր, նազելի իմ, զարթի՛ր:

Song

From your royal sleep, wake,
Wake, my gracious one, wake,
The sun has come and reaches out,
Wake, my gracious one, wake.

Lovely picture, oval vision,
Perfect as the full moon—
No one can be found who equals you,
Wake, my gracious one, wake.

The very sight of you possesses me,
Bewitches me, makes me your slave;
And lest you burn beneath the sun,
Wake, my gracious one, wake.

Heartbroken, how long must I cry,
O rose, O unfading red rose?
Only see how pitiful I am,
Wake, my gracious one, wake.

Hot and evil winds swept down,
To burn your tender leaves,
But the dark night has passed now—
Wake, my gracious one, wake.

My noble love is peerless,
Her ring the most precious jewel;
In this year 1708,
Wake, my gracious one, wake.

Սայեաթ Նովա

Sayat-Nova

1712–1795

Աշխարումբս Ա՛խ Չիմ Քաշի

Աշխարումբս ա՛խ չիմ քաշի, քանի վուր ջա՛ն իս ինձ ամա.
Անմահական ջրով լիքը օսկէ փնջան իս ինձ ամա.
Նստիմ, վրէս շուաք անիս՝ գարբաբ վրան իս ինձ ամա.
Սուսա իմացի՛, էնենց սրպանէ՝ սուլթան ուխան իս ինձ ամա:

Մէճկղ սալբ ու չինարի պէս, հանդզ փռանգի ատլաս է,
Լիզուղ շաքար, պռուզղ դանդ, ակռեքըղ մարքըրիտ ալմաս է,
Օսկու մէջը մինա արած, աճկիրըզ ակնակապ թաս է.
Պատուական անգին ջավայիր, լալ-բադեշխան իս ինձ ամա:

Յիս էս դարդին վո՛ւնց դիմանամ՝ մակա՞մ սիրտըս ունիմ քարած,
Արտասունքս արուն շինեցիր, խիլքս գլխէս ունիմ տարած,
Նուր բադ իս, Նուր բադլի մէջը, բոլորքդ վարթով չափարած.
Վրբէղ շուռ գամ բըլբուլի պէս՝ սիրով սէյրան իս ինձ ամա:

Քու էշխըն ինձի մաստ արաւ. յիս գարթուն իմ, սիրտս է քնած.
Աշխարս աշխարով կշտացաւ, իմ սիրտս քիզնից սով մնաց.
Եա՛ր, քիզ ինչո՞վ թարիֆ անիմ՝ աշխարումն բան չմնաց.
Կրակէ ծովեմէն դուս էկած, ռաշ ու ջէյրան իս ինձ ամա:

Ի՛նչ կ՛ուլի մէկ հիղըս խօսիս, թէ վուր Սայեաթ Նովու եար իս.
Շուղկէղ աշխարս բունիլ է՝ արեգագի դէմը փար իս.
Հուտով հիլ, միխակ, դարիչին, վարդ, մանիշակ, սուսանբար իս,
Կարմրագուն՝ դաշտի ծաղիկ, հովտաց շուշան իս ինձ ամա:

I'll Not Cry "Alas"

I'll not cry "alas" to all this world so long as you're the soul of my life.
You are my golden goblet, brimming with immortal water.
When I sit down, you are my shade, you are my gilded canopy,
Discover in what I'm blameworthy, then put me to death—you are
                                  both my sultan and khan.

Your waist is slim as a cypress, your color is French satin,
Your tongue is sweet, your lips are pink candy, and your teeth
                                  are pearls,
Your eyes shine as polished bowls, polished and worked in gold,
Wondrous, priceless gem, you are the very ruby of Badeshkhan.

This suffering—how am I to endure it? Do you think my heart
                                  is stone?
You have made my tears bloody with pain, you have brought me
                                  to the edge.
Yet you are a garden circled with roses.
Would that I could perch near you, like a nightingale—you are lovely
                                  to behold.

Loving you has made me mad—I am awake, but my heart is
                                  dreaming;
Though the world is content with the world, my heart still longs
                                  for you.
Dear one, in what other way can I praise you—there's nothing else in
                                  the world left for me to do?
You are brilliant as a winged horse of fire, my gazelle leapt up
                                  from the sea.

Since you are the one Sayat-Nova loves, why not speak to him
                                  just once?
Your radiance shadows all the world, you are splendid as the sun.
You are cardamon, rose, carnation, violet and soussamber,
You are my lily of the valley, a rose-tinted flower of the field.

The terms *sultan* and *khan* are Turkish and Persian, respectively, and are here used as synonyms for despot or executioner.

Աշխարհս մէ Փանջարա է

Աշխարհս մէ փանջարա է, թաղերումէն բեզարիլ իմ,
Մրտիկ տուողը կու խուցուի, դաղերումէն բեզարիլ իմ.
Էրեգ լաւ էր կանց վուր էսօր, վաղերումէն բեզարիլ իմ.
Մարթ համաշա մէկ չի՛ լի, խաղերումէն բեզարիլ իմ։

Դովլաթը էհտիբար չունէ, յիփ որ կ՚երթայ իր շքարով,
Լաւ մարթն էն է՛ գլուխը պահէ աշխարումըս էհտիբարով.
Աշխարս միզ մնալու չէ՛ իմաստնասիրաց խաբարով.
Գ՚ուզիմ թռչի բլբուլի պէս, բաղերումէն բեզարիլ իմ։

Օ՞վ կ՚ոսէ թէ յիս կու ապրիմ առուտեմէն ինչրու մուտը՝
Աստձու ճեռումը հիշտ է մարթու աշխարք ելումուտը.
Զուրթըս էնդուր ճամբայ չէ գնում՝ շատացիլ է խալխի սուտը.
Քրսանը մէ դող չին պահում, աղերումէն բեզարիլ իմ։

Աշխարս միզ մնալու չէ, քանի նստինք գող ու սափին.
Հուծ կաթնակիր Աթա՛մի գաթ, նա՛լաթ լլի էտ քու բախին.
Համփիրութինըս հատիլ է, չիմ դիմանում խալխի գափին.
Դոստիրըս դուշման ին դառի,— յաղերումէն բեզարիլ իմ։

Սայեաթ Նովէն ասաց՝ դարդըս կանց մէ ճարը շատացիլ է.
Ջունիմ վաղուան քաղցըր փառքս, հիմի դարը շատացիլ է.
Բլբուլի պէս էնդուր դուլամ՝ վարթիս խարը շատացիլ է.
Ջի՛ն թողնում վախտին բացուելու, քաղերումէն բեզարիլ իմ։

The World is a Window

The world's a window—I'm weary of so many windows;
He who looks in them is harmed—I'm tired of so many windows;
Yesterday was better than today—I'm weary of tomorrows;
Man isn't always the same—I'm weary of all the games that
                                                                  are played.

The wealth that can vanish in battle is not to be trusted;
The good man's the one whose conduct is good;
The world will not be left to us, or so say the sages;
I want to fly like the nightingale—I'm weary of the land.

Who says that I must live from morning till dusk?
Man's entry, man's exit is simple work for the hand of God;
Truth no longer walks a straightforward path, and people lie at an
                                                      ever-quickening pace.
Not one in twenty keeps a servant—I'm weary of the whole lot
                                                      of masters.

However much we feast, how much enjoy, the world will not finally
                                                      be left to us:
Childish, milk-fed sons of Adam, I curse you for your feasting.
My patience is gone, I can't stand to see merriment any more;
My friends have become my enemies—I'm weary of all the games that
                                                      are played.

Sayat-Nova said: My troubles have outgrown their remedies;
I can't have tomorrow's sweet glory, the whole world seeks it today—
And so I cry like a nightingale; there are more and more pests on my
                                                      roses,
And they won't let my roses bloom—I'm weary of searching for a
                                                    splendid one to pick.

Ղեւոնդ Ալիշան
Ghevond Alishan
1820–1901

Հրազդան

Հրազդա՜ն, գետակդ իմ հայրենի,
Հրազդա՜ն, ջրիկդ իմ անուշիկ,
Ահա թողել զՀողն օտարի,
Բաբկէնս հասել եմ պանդխտիկ։

    Ա՜յ Հրազդան, ա՜յ ջուրբ Հայրենիք,
    Ա՜յ ափունք, է՞ր կու լայք լուիկ։

Ես ձեր դրացենակն եմ, չէ՞ք ճանչել,
Սիրտս բղձեզ չէ մոոցել իսկի.
Դուք կարկըչիկդ է՞ր էք մոոցել,
Ծիծղուն երեսդ է՞ր սուգ ունի։

    Ա՜յ Հրազդան, ա՜յ ջուրբ Հայրենիք,
    Ա՜յ ափունք, է՞ր կու լայք լուիկ։

Վա՜հ, մեր կանաչ անտառիկս ո՞ւր,
Ո՞ւր տաղաւարիկս, ո՞ւր մեր նչիս,
Հովո՞ւն եղան, թէ ծովուն կուլ.
Ո՞ւր մեր տնակն, ո՞ւր մեր այգիս։

    Ա՜յ Հրազդան, ա՜յ ջուրբ Հայրենիք,
    Ա՜յ ափունք, է՞ր կու լայք լուիկ։

Ո՞ւր ես, աչիցս լոյս Խանուկ.
Իմ ընկերներն ո՞ւր են, Հրազդան.
Միթէ Պարսկի՞ն եղան գերուկ,
Միթէ ամէնքն ի հո՜ղ մտան։

    Ա՜յ Հրազդան, ա՜յ ջուրբ Հայրենիք,
    Ա՜յ ափունք, է՞ր կու լայք լուիկ։

Ա՜հ, անցուցնաց եղել ամէն.
Ա՜յ, անցուցնաց է Հայաստան.
Զիս անմէկիկ թողած ասաէն,
Ետ անցնիս, գնաս դո՛ւն այլ Հրազդան...,
Անցի՛ր, գնա՛, ջրիկդ հայրենի,
Արտասունք հերիք են բաբկենի։

Hrazdan

Hrazdan, river of my homeland,
Hrazdan, my small sweet river,
O, you've quit the foreign lands
And brought my Papken to his home.

> O Hrazdan, O waters of my homeland,
> O banks, must you hold this sorrow?

Don't you remember I'm your neighbor?
My heart has certainly not forgotten you,
But where is your gentle voice now?
Your sparkling face—must it still look so sad?

> O Hrazdan, O waters of my homeland,
> O banks, must you hold this sorrow?

O where, now, is our stand of greenwood,
Our delicate arbor, our almond tree?
Have these been plundered by the wind or the sea?
Where is our cottage, where is our field?

> O Hrazdan, O waters of my homeland,
> O banks, must you hold this sorrow?

Where is the joy of my sight, the wild lily?
And where are all my friends, Hrazdan?
Could the Persians have taken them captive?
Could they have joined the dust, one and all?

> O Hrazdan, O waters of my homeland,
> O banks, must you hold this sorrow?

O, Armenia too has vanished!
Now that you have left me here alone,
You must go too, and take me with you, Hrazdan—
Flow on, flow away, waters of my homeland,
Enough—Papken has shed tears enough.

Միքայէլ Նալբանդեան
Michael Nalbandian
1829–1866

Ազատութիւն

Ազատ Աստուածն այն օրից,
Երբ հաճեցաւ շունչ փչել,
Իմ հողանիւթ շինուածքին
Կենդանութիւն պարգեւել.

Ես անբարբառ մի մանուկ
Երկու ձեռքս պարգեցի,
Եւ իմ անգօր թեւերով
Ազատութիւնն գրկեցի։

Մինչ գիշերը անհանգիստ
Օրօրոցում կապկապած
Լալիս էի անդադար,
Մօրս քունը խանգարած,

Խնդրում էի նորանից
Բազուկներս արձակել.
Ես այն օրից ուխտեցի
Ազատութիւնը սիրել։

Թոթով լեզուս մինչ կապեր
Արձակուեցան, բացուեցան,
Մինչ ծնողքըս իմ ճայնից
Խնդացին ու բերկրեցան,

Նախկին խօսքն, որ ասացի,
Չէր Հայր, կամ մայր, կամ այլ ինչ.
Ազատութի՛ւն, դուրս թռաւ
Իմ մանկական բերանից։

«Ազատութի՞ւն», ինձ կրկնեց
Ճակատագիրն վերեւից.
«Ազատութեա՞ն դու գինուոր
Կամիս գրուիլ այս օրից։

Ո՛հ, փշոտ է ճանապարհդ,
Քեզ շատ փորձանք կը սպասէ.
Ազատութիւն սիրողին
Այս աշխարհը խիստ նեղ է»։

Freedom

From the day that God, serene and unconstrained,
Was pleased to course His breath
Into my earthly elements
And grant me my life,

I, an infant, too young to speak,
Lifted my arms,
And with my weak new hands
Grasped Freedom.

Restless at night,
Swaddled in my cradle,
I cried endlessly,
Disturbing my mother's sleep;

I constantly begged her
To release my arms,
And from that day on I vowed
To love Freedom.

As the restraints on my stammering tongue
Began to loosen, to unbind,
As my parents smiled
And grew joyful at my voice,

The very first word I cried out
Was not father, nor mother nor anything else:
Freedom leaped out
Of my innocent mouth.

Above me Destiny
Repeated *"Freedom?*
Would you like to be a soldier,
From this day on, for Freedom?

"O your path will be rock-strewn,
Many mishaps lie in the way;
For the one who loves freedom
This world is a narrow road."

—Ազատութի՛ւն, — գոչեցի, —
Թող որոտայ իմ գլխին
Փայլակ, կայծակ, Հուր, երկաթ,
Թող դառ դէն թշնամին,

Ես մինչ ի մահ, կախաղան,
Մինչեւ անարգ մահու սիւն,
Պիտի գոռամ, պիտ կրկնեմ
Անդադար, «Ազատութի՛ւն»։

"Freedom!" I called out,
"Let lightning, fire, flares, and iron
Burst over my head,
Let the enemy plot—

"Until death, until the gallows,
Until dropped from the scaffold of death,
I will shout out over and over,
Endlessly, Freedom!"

Մկրտիչ Պէշիկթաշլեան

Mgrdich Beshiktashlian
1829–1868

Գարուն

Օ՛հ, ի՛նչ անուշ եւ ի՛նչապէս գով
Առաւօտուց փչես, Հովի՛կ,
Ծաղկանց վրայ գուրգուրալով
Եւ մագերուն կուսին փափկիկ,
Բայց չե՛ս Հովիկ իմ Հայրենեաց,
Գնա՛, անցի՛ր սրտէս ի բաց։

Օ՛հ, ի՛նչ աղու եւ սրտագին
Ծառոց մէջէն երգես, Թռչնի՛կ.
Սիրոյ ժամերն ի յանտառին
Զմայլեցան ի քո ձայնիկ.
Բայց չե՛ս Թռչնիկ իմ Հայրենեաց,
Գնա՛, երգէ՛ սրտէս ի բաց։

Օ՛հ, ի՛նչ մրմունջ հանես, վտա՛կ,
Ականակիտ ու հանդարտիկ,
Քու հայելոյդ մէջ անապակ
Նային գիրենք վարդն ու աղջիկ.
Բայց չես վտակ իմ Հայրենեաց,
Գնա՛, հոսէ՛ սրտէս ի բաց։

Թէպէտ Թռչնիկն ու հովն հայոց
Ալեբակաց շրջին վերայ,
Թէպէտ աղտոր վտակն հայոց
Նօճիներու մէջ կը սողայ,
Նոքա հարա՛ժք են Հայրենեաց,
Նոքա չերթա՛ն սրտէս ի բաց։

Spring

O mild breeze, all through the early morning
You blow so gently, so soft, so cool,
Tenderly over the flowers
Over the maiden's fine-spun hair.
Yet if you're not a breeze from my homeland,
Pass on and away from my heart, be gone.

O bird in the leaf-heavy trees
You sing so sweetly, piercing and true,
Indeed the Love-hours in the forest
Admire your long and ardent trilling.
Yet if you're not a bird from my homeland,
Pass on, fly away from my heart, be gone.

O clear and peaceful little river
Your whispers rising from the banks are soft,
And the rose and the maiden
Are mirrored so well by your tranquil face.
Yet if you're not a brook from my homeland,
Pass on, flow away from my heart, be gone.

Though the mild breeze and the fair bird of Armenia
Hover now only over ruins,
And though the murky brook of Armenia
Winds its way among cypresses,
These are the very sounds of my homeland
May these never pass from my heart.

Love-hours may be a personification of the time that lovers have enjoyed together in the forest.

Ռափայէլ Պատկանեան

Rapael Patkanian
1830–1882

Օրօրոցի երգ

Արի՛, ի՛մ սոխակ, թո՛ղ պարտէզ մերին,
Տաղերով քուն բե՛ր տղիս աչերին․
Բայց նա լալիս է․ դու, սոխակ, մի՛ գալ,
Իմ որդին չ՚ուզէ տիրացու դառնալ։

Ե՛կ, աբեղաձա՛գ, թո՛ղ արտ ու արոտ,
Օրորէ՛ տղիս, քնի է կարօտ․
Բայց նա լալիս է․ դու, ճագուկ, մի՛ գալ,
Իմ որդին չ՚ուզէ աբեղայ դառնալ։

Թո՛ղ դու, տատրակի՛կ, քու ճագն ու քունը,
Վուվուլով տղիս բե՛ր անուշ քունը․
Բայց նա լալիս է․ տատրակի՛կ, մի՛ գալ,
Իմ որդին չ՚ուզէ սգաւոր դառնալ։

Կաչաղա՛կ ճարպիկ, գո՛ղ, արծաթասէր,
Շահի զրուցով որդուս քունը բեր․
Բայց նա լալիս է․ կաչաղա՛կ, մի՛ գալ,
Իմ որդին չ՚ուզէ սովդաքար դառնալ։

Թո՛ղ որսորդ, արի՛, քաջասի՛րտ բազէ,
Քու երգը գուցէ իմ որդին կ՚ուզէ․․․
Բազէն որ եկաւ՝ որդիս լռեցաւ․
Իրազմի երգերի ձայնով քնեցաւ։

Cradle Song

Come, nightingale, leave our garden,
With your songs bring sleep to my son's eyes;
But now he cries, don't come, nightingale,
My child doesn't wish to be a deacon.

Come, monk-child, let hill and valley
Rock my son, he's in need of sleep;
But now he cries, don't come, O monk-child,
My child doesn't wish to be a monk.

Turtledove, leave your young and your nest,
And with your cooing bring gentle sleep to my son;
But now he cries, don't come, O turtledove,
My son doesn't wish to be a mourner.

Magpie, silver-loving, thieving, clever one,
Bring sleep to my son with a story of profit;
But now he cries, don't come, magpie,
My son doesn't wish to be a dealer.

Come, brave falcon, quit your prey,
Maybe my son will favor your song . . .
When the falcon appeared my son fell still,
And slept to the sound of battle songs.

Monk-child is a term of endearment, used colloquially.
The *magpie* is a traditional symbol of greed and acquisitiveness.

Վարդանի երգը

Հիմի է՞լ լռենք, եղբարք, հիմի է՞լ,
Երբ մեր թշնամին իր սուրն է դրել,
Իր օրհասական սուրը մեր կրծքին,
Ականջ չի դնում մեր լաց ու կոծին.
Ասացէ'ք, եղբարք հայեր, ի՞նչ անենք, —
             Հիմի է՞լ լռենք:

Հիմի է՞լ լռենք, երբ մեր թշնամին,
Դաւով, հրապուրքով տիրեց մեր երկրին,
Ջնջեց աշխարհից Հայկայ անունը,
Հիմքից կործանեց Թորգոմայ տունը,
Խլեց մեզանից թագ, և'լ խոսք, և'լ գէնք, —
             Հիմի է՞լ լռենք:

Հիմի է՞լ լռենք, երբ մեր թշնամին
Խլեց մեր սուրբը — պաշտպան մեր անձին,
Մշակի ձեռքիցն էլ խոփը խլեց,
Այդ սուրբ ու խոփից մեր շղթան կռեց,
Վա՜յ մեզ, շղթայով կապած գերի ենք, —
             Հիմի է՞լ լռենք:

Հիմի է՞լ լռենք, երբ մեր թշնամին՝
Սոսկալի գէնքը բռնած մեր գլխին,
Կուլ տալ է տալիս արտասուք առատ,
Ադեխարշ բողոք վարուց ապիրատ.
Մեր գլուխ լալու Եփրատ ո՞ւր պտտենք, —
             Հիմի է՞լ լռենք:

Հիմի է՞լ լռենք, երբ մեր թշնամին
Լիրբ գողոզութեամբ լցրած իր հոգին,
Արդարութեան ճայնն հանած իր սրտից
Արտաքսում է մեզ մեր բնիկ երկրից,
Պանդո'խտ, հալածեա'լ, եղբարք, ո՞ւր դիմենք, —
             Հիմի է՞լ լռենք:

Vartan's Song

Even now, brothers, shall we still be silent, shall we?
When our enemy has placed his sword,
His fateful sword against our hearts,
And will not hear our cries and lamentation,
Say, my Armenian brothers, what should we do?
    Shall we still be silent?

Even now, shall we still be silent when our enemy,
Using unctuous words and treachery, takes away the land
That once belonged to us, sweeping from the earth the name
Of Haig and burning the House of Torkom to the ground,
Robbing us of our crown, our speech, our weapons—
    Shall we still be silent?

Even now, shall we still be silent when our enemy
Grabs our swords—the defense of our lives,
Snatches the plow from the tiller's hand,
And from our plow and our sword forges a chain—
Woe unto us! We are no more than chainbound slaves.
    Shall we still be silent?

Even now, shall we still be silent when our enemy
Holds his awful sword above our heads,
And makes us swallow our endless river of tears
—Our ancient litany of woeful complaint—
How shall we reach the Euphrates to weep our fill?
    Shall we still be silent?

  Even now, shall we still be silent when our enemy,
His soul grown huge with arrogance,
Shuts the voice of justice out of his heart,
And uproots us from our homeland?
Exiled, persecuted, O brothers, now where shall we appeal?
    Shall we still be silent?

Vartan Mamikonian also known as Vartan the Brave, led the Armenians against the Persians in A.D. 451; he and his forces were martyred in the defense of Christianity. *Haig* was the legendary founder of Armenia; the *House of Torkom*, referred to in the Old Testament, was an ancient royal house. According to Moses of Khoren, Haig was the son of Torkom.

Հիմի է՞լ լռենք, երբ մեր թշնամին,
Անգոհ մեր բերած ծանր զոհերին,
Իւր լիրբ, նզոված ձեռքը կարկառեց,
Ազգութեանս վերջին կապը պատառեց.
Հայի կորուստը մօտ է, ի'նչ անենք, —
            Հիմի է՞լ լռենք:

Հիմի՞ էլ լռենք, երբ մեր թշնամին,
Արհամարհելով մեր փառքն ազգային,
Մեր եկեղեցուն ճռնամերձ եղաւ,
Գառնագզեստ գայլին մեզ գլուխ դրաւ.
Սուրբ խորան յունինք, արդ ո՞ւր աղօթենք, —
            Հիմի է՞լ լռենք:

Հիմի է՞լ լռենք, մարդիկ ի'նչ կ'ասեն,
Երբ մեր տեղ քարինք, ապառաժք խօսեն.
Չէ՞ն ասիլ, որ Հայք արժանի էին
Այդ ստրկական անարգ վիճակին.
Մեր սուրբ քաջ նախնեաց գործերը գիտե'նք, —
            Միևնել ե՞րբ լռենք:

Թող լւչ' մունջը, անդամալոյծը,
Կամ՝ որոց քաղցր է թշնամու լուծը.
Բայց մենք, որ ունինք հոգի ու սիրտ քաջ,
Ե'կ, անվախ ելնենք թշնամու առաջ,
Գոնէ մեր փառքը մահով ետ խլենք —
            Ու այնպէ'ս լռենք:

Even now, shall we still be silent when our enemy,
Unmoved by all the deaths he's made,
Reaches out his cruel, cursed hand
And tears at the last shred of our nation—
We have almost lost Armenia: what shall we do?
    Shall we still be silent?

Even now, shall we still be silent when our enemy,
Disdaining the glory of our nation,
Lays his hands on our sacred church,
And throws us to a pack of wolves, telling us they're sheep;
We have no holy altar, where shall we say our prayers now?
    Shall we still be silent?

Even now, shall we still be silent? What will men say
When even the rocks and cliffs speak out, instead of us?
Won't they say Armenians deserve
The shameful life of slaves?
We remember the brave deeds of our honored fathers—
    How much longer shall we be silent?

Let the mute be silent, or the maimed,
Or those who find the enemy's burden light;
But we, who have strong hearts and our souls,
Let us rise now, go fearless against our enemy,
At least we may reclaim glory by our death,
    And so be silent in that way.

Գէորգ Դոդոխեան

Gevork Dodokhian

1830–1908

Ծիծեռնակ

Ծիծեռնա'կ, ծիծեռնա'կ,
Դու՝ գարնան սիրո'ւն թռչնակ.
Դէպի ո°ւր, ինձ ասա',
Թռչում ես այդպէս արագ։

Ա'խ, թռի'ր, ծիծեռնակ,
Ծնած տեղդ՝ Աշտարակ.
Անդ չինիր քո բունը
Հայրենի կտուրի տակ։

Անդ Հեռու, ալեւոր
Հայր ունիմ սգաւոր,
Որ միակ իր որդուն
Սպասում է օրէ օր։

Երբ տեսնես դու նրան՝
Ինձնից շատ բարեւ արա',
Ասա', թող նստի լայ
Իւր անբախդ որդու վրայ։

Դու պատմէ, թէ ինչպէ'ս
Աստ անտէր ու խեղճ եմ ես,
Միշտ լալով, ողբալով՝
Կեանքս մաշուել, եղել է կէս։

Ինձ համար ցերեկը
Սուէ է շրջում արեգը,
Գիշերը թաց աչքիս
Քունը մօտ չի գալիս։

Ասի'ր, որ չի բացուած
Թառամեցայ միայնացած,
Ես ծաղիկ գեղեցիկ,
Հայրենի հողից զրկուած։

Դէ'հ, սիրո'ւն ծիծեռնակ,
Հեռացի'ր, թռի'ր արագ
Դէպի Հայոց երկիրը՝
Ծնած տեղդ՝ Աշտարակ։

Swallow

Swallow, swallow,
Fine bird of spring,
Tell me, where
Are you flying, so fast?

Ah swallow, fly
To Ashtarak, where I was born,
Weave your nest there
Beneath your native roof.

There, far away, I have
An ageing father who mourns,
Who waits out the days
For his only son.

When you see him
Bring him all my love;
Tell him he must sit and weep
Over his luckless son.

Tell him that I'm
Bereft and miserable,
Always crying, always wretched,
My life worn down, half gone.

For me, the day
Passes in darkness,
And no sleep comforts
My eyes at night.

Tell him I am fading
Before I ever came to bloom,
A splendid small flower
Wrenched from its native ground.

Well, pretty swallow,
Be gone, fly away fast
To the land of Armenia,
To Ashtarak, where I was born.

Րաֆֆի (Յակոբ Մելիք-Յակոբեան)
Raffi (Hagop Melik-Hagopian)
1835–1888

Զա՛յն Տուր, Ո՛վ Ծովակ...

Զա՛յն տուր, ով ծովակ, ինչո՞ւ լռում ես.
Ողբակից լինել չկամի՞ս դժբախտիս:
Շարժեցէ՛ք, գեփիւրք, ալիքը վեռ-վեռ.
Խառնէք արտասուքս այս ջրերիս հետ:

Հայաստանի մէջ անցքերին վկայ,
Սկզբից մինչ այժմ, խնդրեմ, ինձ ասա՛.
Մի՞թէ միշտ այսպէս կը մնայ Հայաստան՝
Փշալից անապատ, երբեմն բուրաստան:

Մի՞թէ միշտ այդպէս ազգը խղճալի,
Կը լինի ծառայ օտար իշխանի,
Մի՞թէ Աստուծոյ աթոռի մօտին
Անարժան է Հայն եւ Հայի որդին:

Արդեօք պայո՞ւծ է մի օր, ժամանակ,
Տեսնել Մասիսի գլխին մի դրօշակ,
Եւ ամէն կողմից պանդուխտ Հայազգիք
Դիմել դէպ իւրեանց սիրուն Հայրենիք:

Դժուար այդ․ միայն, տեսուչըղ վերին,
Կենդանացրո՛ւ Հայութեան հոգին,
Ծագի՛ր նոցա դուքո լոյս գիտութեան,
Որով իբր եակ նոքա բանական,
Կը ճանչեն մարդուս կեանքի խորհուրդը,
Կը լինին գործովք տիրոջ փառաբան:

Little Lake

Little lake, speak up, why are you silent?
Won't you grieve with someone as hapless as me?
O winds, stir the water to moving,
And with the water mix my tears.

Witness of what has happened in Armenia,
Please tell me all, from beginning to end—
Will Armenia, once a fragrant land,
Be always as now, a barren wilderness?

Will our tormented nation always as now
Be subject to a foreign prince?
Must Armenians and their sons
Be found unworthy to stand beside God's throne?

Will our day, our time, never come,
When a flag stands high on the peak of Massis
And from far and near exiled Armenians
Return to their own fragrant land?

Unlikely that will come to pass; only you,
O Lord, can breathe life into the Armenian spirit,
And shine the light of wisdom upon it—
And by it, truly alive then and aware,
Armenians can discover what has meaning
And by their deeds glorify the Lord.

Massis, long the symbol of Armenia, represents both freedom and awesome beauty. As a geographical term, it is applied generically to the Massisian mountains, including the fabled Mt. Ararat.

Ղազարոս Աղայեան
Ghazaros Aghayan
1840–1911

Յիշողութիւն

Ծիծեռնակը բոյն էր շինում,
Ե՛լ շինում էր, ե՛լ երգում,
Ամէն մի շիղ կպցնելիս՝
Առաջուան բոյնն էր յիշում։

Մէկ անգամ էր նա բոյն շինել
Եւ շատ անգամ կարկատել,
Բայց այս անգամ վերադարձին
Բոյնն աւերակ էր գտել։

Այժմ նորից բոյն էր շինում,
Ե՛լ շինում էր, ե՛լ երգում,
Ամէն մի շիղ կպցնելիս՝
Առաջուան բոյնն էր յիշում։

Նա յիշում էր անցած տարին
Իր սնուցած ձագերին,
Որոնց ճամբին յափշտակեց
Արիւնարբու թշնամին։

Բայց նա կրկին բոյն էր շինում,
Ե՛լ շինում էր, ե՛լ երգում,
Ամէն մի շիղ կպցնելիս՝
Առաջուան բոյնն էր յիշում։

Remembrance

The swallow is building a nest,
Building a nest and singing,
And every time she places a straw,
She remembers her former nest.

Only once before she built a nest
But she mended it many times,
And then, the last time she returned,
She found the nest in ruin.

But now she is building a nest again,
Building a nest and singing,
And every time she places a straw,
She remembers her former nest.

She remembers, too, the past year,
When, as she gathered food for her young,
The bloodthirsty enemy
Snatched them all from the road.

But once again she is building a nest,
Building a nest and singing,
And every time she places a straw,
She remembers her former nest.

Ջիւանի (Սերոբ Լեւոնեան)
Jivani (Serop Levonian)
1846–1909

Կուգան Ու Կ'երթան

Զախորդ օրերը ճմման նման կու գան ու կ'երթան,
Վհատելու չէ', վերջ կ'ունենան, կու գան ու կ'երթան.
Դառն ցաւերը մարդու վերայ չեն մնայ երկար,
Որպէս յածախորդ շարուէ-շարան կու գան ու կ'երթան։

Փորձանք, հալածանք եւ նեղութիւն ազգերի գլխից,
Ինչպէս ճանապարհի քարաւան՝ կու գան ու կ'երթան.
Աշխարհը բուրաստան է յատուկ, մարդիկը՝ ծաղիկ,
Ո՛րքան մանուշակ, վարդ, բալասան կու գան ու կ'երթան։

Ո՛չ ուժեղը թող պարծենայ, ո'չ տկարը տխրի,
Փոփոխակի անցքեր զանազան կու գան ու կ'երթան.
Արեւը առանց վախենալու ցայտում է լոյսը,
Ամպերը դէպի աղօթարան կու գան ու կ'երթան։

Երկիրը ուսեալ գալակին է փայփայում մօր պէս.
Անկիրթ ցեղերը թաթարական կու գան ու կ'երթան,
Աշխարհը հիւրանոց է, Ջիւան, մարդիկը հիւր են,
Այսպէս է կանոնը բնական, կու գան ու կ'երթան։

They Come and Go

The sad days, like winter, come and go,
Don't despair: they'll have an end, they'll come and go;
Bitter pains do not stay long with man,
Like customers in a store, they come and go.

Calamity, persecution, bleak times, the fate of nations:
Like caravans on a journey, they come and go;
The world's a fragrant, wild garden, man its flowers,
The violets, roses, balsam come and go.

The strong should not be proud, nor the weak sad:
The shifting strong currents come and go;
The fearless sun throws down its light,
The clouds, gathered in heaven for prayer, come and go.

The world makes over its learned ones, as a mother her child,
The savage, stray races, they come and go;
The world's an inn, Jivan, and man is the guest,
Such is the way of nature, they come and go.

Պետրոս Դուրեան
Bedros Tourian
1852–1872

Իմ Մահը

Եթէ տժգոյն մահու հրեշտակ
Անհուն ժպտով մ՚իջնէ իմ դէմ,
Շոգինան ցաւքս ու հոգիս,
Գիւցէ՛ք, որ դեռ կենդանի եմ։

Եթէ սնարըս ի՚մ տիպար՝
Մոմ մը վառտ ու մահադէմ,
Ո՛հ, նշուլէ ցուրտ ճառագայթ,
Գիւցէ՛ք, որ դեռ կենդանի եմ։

Եթէ ճակտովս արտօսրաթոծ՝
Զիս պատանի մէջ ցուրտ զերթ վէմ
Փաթթեն, դնեն սեւ դագաղը,
Գիւցէ՛ք, որ դեռ կենդանի եմ։

Եթէ հնչէ տխուր կոչնակ,
Թրթռուն ծիծաղն մահու դժխեմ,
Դագաղս առնէ իր յամր քայլ,
Գիւցէ՛ք, որ դեռ կենդանի եմ։

Եթէ մարդիկն այն մահերգակ,
Որք սեւ ունին ու խոժոռ դէմ,
Համափռեն խունկ ու աղօթք,
Գիւցէ՛ք, որ դեռ կենդանի եմ։

Եթ՚ յարդարեն իմ հողակոյտ,
Եւ հեծեծմամբ ու սգալէն
Իմ սիրելիքը բաժնուին,
Գիւցէ՛ք, որ մի՛շտ կենդանի եմ։

Իսկ աննշան եթէ մնայ
Երկրի մէկ խորշն հողակոյտն իմ,
Եւ լիշատա՛կս ալ թառամի,
Ա՛հ, այն ատե՛ն ես կը մեռնիմ։

My Death

When the pallid angel of death
Comes to me with his impenetrable smile,
And my pain begins to dissolve, my soul,
Know that I'm still alive.

When shining down from the head of my bed,
A dim small candle lights my dying face,
And gives off only a bitter cold ray,
Know that I'm still alive.

When, all wrapped, I am placed in a dark coffin,
And I lie in my layered shroud, a cold stone,
My brow now tearless and sanctified,
Know that I'm still alive.

When the peal of the iron bell
Causes a smile on the face of death,
And my coffin makes its silent way,
Know that I'm still alive.

When those men who chant the deathsongs,
Who wear black, and have harsh lines in their faces
Give prayers and spread incense all around,
Know that I'm still alive.

When they have trimmed my earthly grave,
And, sobbing and grieving,
Turned homeward my family and friends,
Know that I'm still alive.

But if my grave remains unmarked
In a corner of the earth,
And remembrance of me fades away,
Ah, know then that I am dead.

Ալեքսանդր Ծատուրեան
Alexander Dzadourian
1864–1917

Մի՛ լար, Բլբո՛ւլ

Մի՛ լար, բլբո՛ւլ, քեզ մի՛ տանջիր,
Որ փոթորիկն անիրաւ
Վարդդ սիրուն, վարդդ կարմիր
Թփից պոկե՛ց ու տարա՛ւ...

Կ՚անցնեն օրեր... Կը գայ կրկին
Մի նո՛ր գարուն վարդաբեր.
Եւ մոռացած քո վիշտը հին,
Նորից կ՚երգես վարդին սէր:

Բայց վա՛յ կեանքի այն խեղճ երգչին,
Որ վաղաժամ որբացած,
Իւր սիրելի խսուն վարդին
Ցուրտ հողին է նա յանձնած...

Երգչի համար գարուն չի՛ գայ,
Ո՛չ նա նոր վարդ կը սիրէ.
Նա պէտք է լայ, պէտք է սգայ,
Մինչ յաւիտեան կը լռէ...

Don't Cry, Bulbul

Don't you cry, bulbul, don't you droop
    Because the cold storm
Tore off and carried away from the bush
    The beautiful rose, the red rose.

Days will pass—it will return again,
    A new spring, a rose-bearing spring,
And having forgotten the old pain,
    You'll sing of love to the rose again.

But O, for the singer of life,
    Orphaned in early years,
Who commits to the hard earth
    His lovely, beloved rose:

No spring is in store for the singer,
    For he cannot love a new rose—
He must weep, he must mourn
    Until he sings no more.

Յովհաննէս Յովհաննիսեան
Hovhanness Hovhanissian
1864–1929

Ա՛խ, Տուէ՛ք ինձ

Ա՛խ, տուէ՛ք ինձ քաղցըր մի քուն,
Կեանքից Հեռո՛ւ սլանամ
Այն աշխարհը, ուր խնդութիւն,
Ուր սէրն է միշտ անթառամ։

Քնքուշ վարդերն ինձ բարձ լինին,
Վառ կանաչից իմ վերմակ,
Նոցա բոյրը զուարթագին
Ծծեմ անվերջ ես անյագ։

Եւ խայտալով իմ առաջին
Վտակն անուշ խոխոջէ,
Մի թարմութիւն եդեմային
Զուրս բոլորքս տարածէ։

Եւ ինձ ժպտի արշալոյսին
Գարնան մատաղ ալեգակ,
Եւ գիշերով իմ ճակատին
Խաղայ գողտրիկ վառ լուսնակ։

Եւ աչագեղ կոյսն ականջիս
Իւր մեղեղին մեղմ Հնչէ,
Եւ Հերարձակ՝ սիրով վզիս
Փարէ քնքուշ, փաղաքշէ...

Եւ յաւիտեան վայելչութիւն
Գրկէ Հոգիս, յյագենամ...
Ա՛խ, տուէ՛ք ինձ քաղցըր մի քուն,
Հեռո՛ւ, Հեռո՛ւ սլանամ։

A Gentle Sleep

Ah, give me a gentle sleep
So I may drift far away from life
To a world where laughter,
Where love are always bright.

Let delicate roses be my pillow,
The soft new grass my bed,
And their fresh young fragrance
Let me always breathe with joy.

And before me, brilliantly,
Let the clear stream flash,
And, like Eden, spread
Freshness all around me.

And may dawn find gladness for me
In the tender sun of spring,
And at night let the gleaming moon
Move slowly across my brow.

And may the silken-eyed maiden
Lilt her song at my ear,
And, dishevelled, dally at my neck
Tenderly, lovingly, caressingly . . .

And may eternal happiness
Embrace my soul—unquenched I go—
Ah, grant me a gentle sleep
That I may drift away, far away.

Յակոբ Յակոբեան

Hakop Hakopian

1866–1937

Իմ Աշխարհը

Որքա՜ն էլ ուզեմ ձգտել դեպի ձեզ,
　　Վեհապանծ սարեր,
Ու փարուժել մաքուր ձեր ճիւնեայ կրծքին,
　　Որքա՜ն ուզեմ ես
　　Սլանալ վեր-վեր,
Արծիւի նման հպարտ սաւառնել՝
　　Չլի՞ չե՛մ կարող, կուսական լեռներ,
　　Երկիրը թողնել,
Որ խարխափում է կեղտ ու մութի մէջ,
　　Տառապում անվերջ․
Եւ ես կարիքի աշխարհքն եմ ընտրում —
　　Ճնշուած ու լքուած,
Ուր վիշտն ու գրկանք իրար հետ գրկուած՝
　　Մի ելք եմ փնտռում։
Եւ դուք վա՛ ո ասողեր,
　　Որքա՜ն էլ դիւթող,
Սիրտը պարուրող լինի ձեր հմայք՝
Որքա՜ն էլ գերէք հոգիս երազող
Ու ինձ երկնային տանէք ձեր աշխա՛րհք՝
　　Դարձեալ չե՛մ կարող․
Կապուած եմ կամայ իմ մայր հողի հետ։
Ցար ու յարատեւ ամբոխի լացը,
　　Ցաւ ու կսկիծը,
Ինձ կոչ են անում, թէ՝ արի՛, պոէտ,
　　Մեր վիշտը լացիր,
　　Մեզ ընկե՛ր դարձիր։
Օ՛, ինչպէ՜ս քաղցր է երկինք վերանալ,
　　Վիշտ, հոգս մոռանալ,
Լուսնի փայլի մէջ լողալ սաւառնիլ,
　　Աստղերը գրկել,
Բայց եւ անողոք իրականութեան
　　Ուրուականը սև,
　　Որպէս մի ժանտ դեւ,
Մարմնացած ըմբոստ բողոքի նման
　　Տալիս է հրաման․
—«Իջի՛ր երազկոտ երկնային պահից
　　Կեանքին մօտնալու,
Նրան երգ ունիս, վէրք ունիս տալու»։

My Land

However much I wish to climb to your heights,
    Magnificent mountains,
And hold tightly to your fresh and snow-covered sides;
    However much I wish
    To fly up and higher,
Climb the air like an eagle,
O untried mountains, I can't
    Forsake my land,
That wallows in filth and despair,
    Suffering without end;
I must choose the earth of the needy,
    The oppressed and forlorn,
Where pain and deprivation, clinging together,
    Seek a way out.
And you, bright stars,
    However potent your magic,
Your rapturous gleaming,
However you capture my dreaming soul
And carry me far to your heaven-world,
    Yet I cannot, I cannot leave my land—
By my own will I'm bound to my homeland,
To the unending cry of my people,
    To their grief and sorrow.
They call out to me:
    "Come, poet,
    Sing our sorrow,
    Become our friend."
Oh, how good it is to fly up to the sky,
    Forget pain and hardship;
To float and soar beneath the brightness of the moon,
    And touch the stars—
But the gaunt wraith
Of our bleak life,
An evil spirit
Alive with warning and protest,
Issues commands:
"Come down from your dream of heaven,
    Become one with life,
    You have songs of pain to give it."

Ու պիտի իջնեմ... ամբոխից փախս տալ
    Դժուա՛ր է, դժուա՛ր․
Հոգիս ծվլված է նրա հոգու մէջ,
Չզերս կապված նրա չզերին։
    Մի ա՛յլ ճանապարհ
Գոյութիւն չունի երբեք ինձ համար,
Եւ որքան դիւթո՛ղ լինի ձեր համայք,
    Երկի՛նք ու աստղեր,
Կայ մի քրտնալի, կարիքի՛ աշխարհք
    Ճնշուած ու լքուած՝
    Նրա՛ն եմ ընտրում,
Այնտեղ վիշտ, գրկանք իրար հետ գրկուած՝
    Մի ե՛լք են փնտռում...։

And I will come down—it is hard
To ignore my people, it is hard.
My soul is scattered among my people,
My nerves are woven with their nerves.
      No other path
Can lead to meaning for me ever,
And however much your charms allure,
      Oh heaven and stars,
There lives a browbeaten, needy world,
      Oppressed, forlorn
         It is that earth I choose—
There, clinging together, grief and want
      Seek a way out.

Յովհաննէս Թումանեան

Hovhanness Toumanian
1869–1923

Հայոց Վիշտը

Հայոց վիշտը անհուն մի ծով,
Խավար մի ծով ահագին,
էն սև ծովում տառապելով,
Լող է տալիս իմ հոգին:

Մերթ զայրացկոտ ծառս է լինում
Մինչև երկինք կապուտակ,
Ու մերթ յոգնած սուզվում, իջնում
Դեպի խորքերն անյատակ:

Ո՛չ յատակն է գտնում անվերջ
Ու ո՛չ հասնում երկինքն...
Հայոց վշտի մեծ ծովի մեջ
Տառապում է իմ հոգին:

Թռչակներ

Երազումս մի մաքի
Մոտրս եկավ հարցմունքի,
—Աստուա'ծ պահի քո որդին,
Ո՞նց էր համը իմ ճագի...

« »

Ի՞նչ իմանաս ստեղծողի գաղտնիքները անմեկին.—
Ընկե'ր տուաւ, իրար կապեց էս աշխարհքում ամէնքին.
Բանաստեղծին թողեց մենակ, մեն ու մենակ իրեն պէս,
Որ իրեն պէս մոթիկ անի ամէն մէկին ու կեանքին:

« »

Կեանքրս արի հրապարա՛կ, ուռքի կոխան ամէնքի.
Խափան, խոպան ու անպտուղ, անցաւ առանց արդիւնքի:
Ինչքան ծաղիկ պիտի բուսնէր, որ չբուսա՛ւ էս հողին...
Ի՞նչ պատասխան պիտի ես տամ հող ու ծաղիկ տուլողին...

The Armenians' Grief

The Armenian grief is a boundless sea,
An immense, dark sea,
In pain, in that black water,
My soul swims aimlessly.

Now it rises up with fury
Toward the clear sky above,
And tired now, it plunges
To the endless depths.

Wine is not unendingly deep
Nor can it raise me as far as the sky . . .
In the vast sea of Armenian sorrow
My tired soul moves, always in grief.

Quatrains

In my dreams a ewe
Came near me and asked:
"May God keep your son—
How did my kid taste?"

<< >>

How can we know the Creator's unknowable mysteries?
He bound together, gave a companion to everyone in the world;
Only he left the poet alone, alone like Himself and apart,
So that he may attend, like Him, to one and to all and to life.

<< >>

I made my life into a village green, walked on by everyone,
Untended, desolate, and barren, it has passed with not one green shoot;
How many flowers could have bloomed from that soil that have not bloomed—
What answer can I give, to the giver of land and flowers?

Սասունցի Դավիթ

I

Առիծ-Մհերը, գարմով դիցազուն
Քառասուն տարի իշխում էր Սասուն.
Իշխում էր աՀեղ, ուՆրա օրով
Հալքն էլ չէր անցնում Սասնայ սարերով.
Սասմայ սարերից չա՛տ ու չատ Հեռու
Թնդում էր նրա Հշչակն աՀարկու,
Պաուսում էր իր փաքն, արսւքն անվեՀեր.
Հազար բերան էր — մի՛ Առիծ Մհեր։

II

Հսպես, աՀալուր առիծի նման,
Սասմայ սարերում նստած էր իշխան
Քառասուն տարի։ Քառասուն տարում
«Ա՛խ» չէր քաշել նա դեռ իրեն օրում.
Բայց Հիմի, երբ որ եկալ ծերացալ,
Էն անսաՀ սիրտը ներս սողաց մի ցալ։
Սկաալ մտածել դիցազուն ծերը.
—Հասել են կեանքիս աշնան օրերը,
Շուտով սեւ Հողին կ'երթամ ես դերի,
Կ'անցնի ծխի պէս փառքը Մհերի,
Կ'անցնեն է'լ անուն, է'լ սարսափ, է'լ աՀ,
Իմ անտէր ու որբ աշխարքի վրայ
Ուտի կը կանգնեն Հազար քաջ ու դեւ...
Մի ժառանգ չունեմ՝ իմ անցման ետեւ
Իմ թուրը կապի, Սասուն պաՀպանի...
Ու միտք էր անում Հական ծերունի։

III

Մի օր էլ՝ էն դորշ յօնքերը կիտած
Երբ միտք էր անում, երկնքից յանկարծ
Մի Հուր-Հրեղէն յայտնուեց քաշին,
Ոտները ամպոտ կանգնեց առաջին:
—Ողջո՛յն, մեծագոր Սասմայ Հակային.
Քու ճայնը Հասալ Աստրծու գաՀին,
Ու շուտով նա քեզ մի զաւակ կը տայ։
Բայց լա՛լ իմանաս, լեռների՛ արքայ,
Օ՛ր օրը որ քեզ ժառանգ է տուել՝
Էն օր կը մեռնէք քուլ կինն էլ, դո՛ւ էլ։

David of Sassoun

I

Lion-Mher of fable and legend
Reigned at Sassoun for forty years;
He reigned with might, and in his day
No flock dared fly over Sassoun's steeps.
Far and away from the Sassoun highlands
His mighty name was rumored;
His fame spoke his glory, his fearsome deeds—
His single name, Lion-Mher.

II

And seated thus like an awesome lion
In the fastnesses of Sassoun, he reigned
As lord for forty years. For forty years
He had never raised a cry of sorrow,
But now, fallen into declining days,
A sting crept into that fearless heart.
And the legend-burdened old one fell to thinking,
"Alas, the autumn days of my life are here,
The black earth will soon claim me as its slave,
The glories of Lion-Mher pass like smoke,
Even my name will pass, terror and fear;
Alas! On my unowned and orphaned world
There will rise a thousand upstarts, braves, and fiends—
Alas, on my passing, no heir will remain
To wear my sword, be protector to Sassoun."
So mused the giant, troubled greybeard.

III

And one day, while his iron-grey brows were knitted,
While he was deep in thought, suddenly, down from the sky
Came a fiery angel; he stood before the giant hero,
His feet wrapped in billowing clouds.
"Greetings to the all-powerful giant of Sassoun!
Your voice has reached to the throne of God,
And soon He shall grant you a child.
But hear me well, O lord of the mountains,
On the day God grants you an heir,
On that very same day you and your wife will die."

—Իր կա'մքը լինի,— ասաւ Մհերը,—
Մենք մահի'նն ենք միշտ ու մահը՝ մե'րը,
Բայց որ աշխարքում ժառանգ ունենանք՝
Մենք էլ նրանով անմեռ կը մնանք։
Հրբեշտակն այստեղ ցոլացաւ նորից,
Ու էս երջանիկ ալետման օրից
Երբ ինք ամիս, ինք ժամն անցաւ,
Առիծ-Մհերը պաւակ ունեցաւ։
Դալիթ անուանեց իրեն կորիւնին։
Կանչեց իր եղբայր Չէնով Օհանին,
Երկիրն ու որդին աւանդեց նրան,
Ու կինն էլ, ինքն էլ էն օրը մեռան։

IV

Էս դարում՝ Մրսրը, անյաղթ ու Հզոր
Մարա-Մելիքն էր նստած Թագաւոր։
Հենց որ իմացաւ՝ էլ Մհեր չկայ,
Վե'ր կացաւ կուլով Սասունի վրայ։
Չէնով Օհանը ահից սարսափած՝
Թշնամու առաջն ելաւ գլխաբաց,
Ադաչանք արաւ, ընկաւ ոտները․
—Դո'ւ եղիր,— ասաւ,— մեր գլխի տէրը,
Ու քու շուաքում քանի որ մենք կանք,
Քու ծառան լինենք, քու խարջը միշտ տանք,
Միայն մեր երկիր քարուքանդ չանես
Ու քաղցըը աչքով մեզ մռիկ անես։
—Չէ',— ասաւ Մելիք,— քու ամբողջ ազգով
Անց պիտի կենաս իմ թրի տակով,
Որ էգուց-էլօր, ի'նչ էլ որ անեմ,
Ո'չ մի սասունցի թուր չառնի իմ դէմ։
Ու գնաց Օհան՝ բոլոր-բովանդակ
Սասունը բերաւ, քաշեց թրի տակ․
Մենակ Դալիթը, ինչ արբին-չարին,
Մօտ չեկաւ դուշման Մելիքի թրին։
Եկան քաշեցին՝ թէ գօրով տանեն,
Թափ տուաւ, մարդկանց գցեց դէս ու դէն,
Փոքրիկ ճկոյթը մի քարի առաւ,
Ապարաժ քարից կրակ դուրս թռաւ։
—Պէք է սպանեմ էս փոքրիկ ծուռի'ն,—
Ասաւ Թագաւորն իրեն մեծերին։
—Թագաւո'ր,— ասին,— դու ջաքան Հզոր,
Թրիդ տակին է ողջ Սասունն էսօր․
Ի՞նչ պէտք է անի քեզ մի երեխայ,

"His will be done," said Lion-Mher, "we are ever
Of death and death of us, but if in this world,
We gain an heir, we remain deathless in him."
Here the fiery angel gained the air once more,
And from that day of joyous tidings,
After nine months passed and nine hours more,
Lion-Mher had a child; and David
He named his cub; he called his brother to him,
Big-voiced Ohan, and bequeathed his lands and heir
To him. That day he died and his dame, too.

IV

And in those times in Egypt a king reigned,
Melik of Musr, unvanquished, and mighty;
When he heard that Lion-Mher was no more,
He marched straight on Sassoun to fight. Ohan
The big-voiced, quaking with fear, came before
The warlike host unhelmeted and bowed,
And fell on his knees, seeking mercy.
"O Melik be master over our heads,"
He said, "and while we live beneath your shadow
May we always be your servants, pay our tribute,
Only do not lay waste our tillage, our lands,
And with a peaceful eye regard us."
"No," roared Melik, "your people must all pass
Beneath my sword and pay homage, so that
Henceforth whatever I will to do, not one
Sassounite may raise his sword against me."
So Ohan went out and gathered all the Sassounites
Together and passed them all beneath the sword;
David alone, despite every move
Tried, did not come near the sword of Melik, his foe.
Vexed, the Sassounites came and tugged at him:
He bolted, scattering the throng here and there,
And meanwhile his little finger grazed a rock
And drew from it a rain of fiery bolts.
To the wise men gathered all around him,
The king said, "I must kill this little fool!"
"O king," they said, "beneath your sword today
All Sassoun stands; surely you alone are mighty here.
What could a mere child do against you,

Թեկուզ իր տեղով Հեևց կրակ դառնայ։
—Դուք գիտէ՛ք, — ասաւ, — Մսրայ Թագաւոր,
Բայց թէ իմ գլխին փորձանք գայ մի օր,
էս ո՛րը վկայ,
Սրանի՛ց կը գայ։

V

էս որ պատահեց, մեր Դաւիթ Հսկան
Մի մանուկ էր դեռ եօթ-ութ տարեկան.
Մանուկ եմ ասում, բայց էնքա՛ն ուժեղ,
Որ նրա համար թէ՛ մարդ, — թէ՛ մժեղ։
Բայց Հնուց խօսք է, մեծ իմաստ ունի,
Թէ խաչը՝ տերը գօրաւոր կ՚անի։
Վա՛յ անտեր որբին աշխարքի վրայ,
Թեկուզ Աուեծի կորի՛ն լինի նա։
Չէնով Օհանը ունէր մի չար կին.
Մին-երկու լռեց, մի օր էլ կարգին
Իրեն մարդու Հետ սկսաւ կռուել.
—Ես մենա՛կ հոգի, հագա՛ր ցավի տեր,
Ի՛նչ ես ուրիշի եթիմը բերել,
Նստեցրել գլխիս պարապ Հացակեր...
Հո՛դեմ գլուխը... ես գիրր, Հօ, չե՛մ
Ամէնքի քէֆի եւեւից թոշեմ...
Մի կուռ կորցրո՛ւ, կարգի՛ր մի բանի,
Գնայ՝ իր համար աշխատանք անի... —
Ու հետն սկսաւ ողբալ ու կոծել,
Իր օրը սգալ, իր բախտն անիծել,
Թէ անբախտ եղաւ աշխարքի միջում,
Ո՛չ մի տեր ունի, ոչ մա՛րդն է խղճում....։
Գնաց Օհանը երեխի ռտի
Մի գոյգ ոտնաման բերաւ երկաթի,
Երկաթի մի կոռ* չալակին դրած,
Ու արաւ Սասմայ քաղքի դառնարած։

VI

Քչեց գառները մեր Հովիւ Հսկան,
Եւաւ Սասունի սարերն աննման։
«է՛յ ջան, սարե՛ր,
Սասման սարե՛ր»...
Որ կանչեց, նրա ձենից աշալոր
Դղորդ-դղմբդմբոցն ընկաւ սար ու ձոր,
Վայրի գազաններ բներից փախան,

Even if he were altogether made of fire, instead?"
"You know best," Egypt's king said, "but if
Harm should fall upon my head some day,
Let this day be witness,
It will come from him."

V

When this event occurred sturdy young David
Was merely a child, seven or eight years old;
I say a child, but one with so much strength
That man or mosquito was the same to him.
But it is an old saying, one with great meaning,
That he who eats soup made of calves' hooves becomes strong.
But, alas! for.the orphan on this earth,
Though he come from the loins of a lion.
Now big-voiced Ohan had a waspish wife;
Once or twice she had held her tongue, but on a certain day
She began to fight thus with her helpmeet:
"I am a lonely soul, heir to a thousand ills,
Why have you brought another's orphan here,
Weighed me down with a useless mouth to feed—
Would that I could cast sod on his head!
I am no handmaid, I, to dance attendance on another!
Find a way to lose him, put him to a task,
Pack him off so he may labor for himself."
Saying this, she began to wail and sob,
To mourn her hapless days, to curse her fate,
That she was luckless on the earth,
That no master did own her, nor pitying spouse.
Ohan set out and brought back a pair
Of iron boots for the child's feet,
Placed an iron staff upon his shoulders,
And made the child shepherd of Sassountown.

VI

The mighty young shepherd drove his flock of sheep
And mounted Sassoun's peerless fastnesses.

> "O endearing highlands,
> Highlands of Sassoun . . ."

When he called, his voice had such force
That the canyons and highlands rang with it,

Քարեքար ընկան, դատարկուն եղան։
Դաւիթը ընկալ նրանց եռեւից,
Որին մի՛ սարից, որին մի՛ ձորից —
Ածուխս, նապաստակ, գայլ, եղնիկ բռնեց,
Հաւաքեց, բերալ, գառներին խառնեց,
Իրիկուան քշեց ողջ Սասմայ քաղաք։
Կաղկա՛նձ ու ոռնո՛ց, աղմո՛ւկ, աղաղա՛կ...
Քաղքըցիք յանկարծ մին էլ էն տեսան՝
Գալիս են Հրէս անհամար գազան.

«Վա՛յ, Հարա՛յ, փախէ՛ք...»
Մեծեր, երեխէք
Սրտաճաք եղած,
Գործներըը թողած,
Որը տուն ընկաւ, որը ժամ, խանութ,
Ու ամուր փակեց դուռն ու լուսամուտ։
Դաւիթը եկալ, կանգնեց մէյդանում.
— Վա՛հ, էս մարդիկը ի՛նչ վաղ են քնում.

Հէ՛յ ուլատէր, Հէ՛յ գառնատէր,
Ելէ՛ք, շուտով բացէք դռներ.

Ով մի՛նն ունէր — տա՛սն եմ բերել,
Ով տա՛սն ունէր — քսա՛նն արել...

Շուտով ելէ՛ք, եկէ՛ք, տարէ՛ք,
Ձեր գառն ու ով գոմերն արէք։

Տեսաւ՝ չեն գալի, դուռ չեն բաց անում,
Ինքն էլ մեկնուեց քաղքի մէյդանում,
Գլուխը դրաւ մի քարի՝ մնաց
Ու մուշ-մուշ քնեց մինչեւ լուսաբաց։
Լուսին իշխաններ եկան միասին,
Գնացին Ջէնով Օհանին ասին.
— Տօ՛ Ջէնով Օհան, տօ՛ մահի տարած,
Էս խենէթը բերիր, արիր գառնարած,
Ո՛չ գառն է ծոկում, ո՛չ գայլն ու աղուէս,
Գազանով լցրեց մեր քաղաքն էսպէս.
Աստուած կը սիրես՝ դի՛ր ուրիշ բանի,
Թէ չէ էս խա՛լխին լեղաճաք կ'անի։

VII

Ելալ Օհանը, Դաւթի մօտ դնաց.

Wild animals sprang from their lairs, scattered
Over the rocks and wandered homeless.
David went after them all, those from the valleys
And those from the hills--fox, hare, wolf, and deer;
He caught these, gathered them, and mixed them with his flock,
And at night he drove them all down to Sassountown.
The noise, the commotion, the dust and the roar,
The charging of numberless beasts let loose:
This the townspeople suddenly saw and heard.

> "Oh! Help! Run!"
> Old and young,
> Panic-stricken,
> Ran away from their chores.

Some ran home, some to church, and some to shops;
All bolted their doors fast and closed the shutters tight.
David boldly entered and stood in the town square:
"Well! How early these people have gone to sleep!

> Ho there! Goat owners, sheep owners,
> Get up swiftly, unbar your doors,
>
> He who had one, I've brought him ten,
> He who had ten, I've brought him scores.
>
> Up, get up swiftly, come and take them,
> Take your sheep and your goats to the barns."

When David saw that no one stirred, no one
Unbarred a door, he placed his head on
A stone, stretched himself out in the square,
And slept soundly till the break of day.
At dawn the burghers rose and together
Went to big-voiced Ohan and said,
"You, big-voiced Ohan, death take you,
It was you who brought this fool and made him herdsman;
He does not part sheep from wolves nor foxes,
And thus he has filled our town with wild beasts.
If you love God, put him to another task,
Or else he'll burst the gall of all these townsfolk."

VII

Ohan arose and went to see David.

—Հորեղբա'յր Օհան, հեռո'ւ եկ, կամա'ց,
Ուլեր կը փախչեն։ — Մին էլ էնտեղից
Մի բոզ նապաստակ, ականջները ցից,
Խրանեց ու ահից դուրս պրծավ յանկարծ։
Դավիթն էր, ելավ, եւետից ընկած
Էն սարը քշեց, էտ բերալ էս ձոր,
Բերավ, ուլերին խառնեց նորից նոր։
—Օ'ֆ, ի'նչ դժար է, Հորեղբայր Օհան.
Աստված օխնել է էն սել-սել ուլեր,
Ամա բոզալուկ էս ուլեր, որ կան,
Փախչում են, վրվում ողջ սարերն ի վեր.
Էնքան եմ երեկ վազել, չարչարվել,
Մինչեւ հալաքել ու տուն եմ բերե'լ...
Նայեց Օհանը, որ Դավթի հագին
Ոտնաման չի էլ մնացել կարգին,
Հահակն է մաշվել, մինչ բուռն է հասել,
Մի օրվայ միջում էնքան է վազել։
—Դավի'թ ջան, — ասավ, — չեմ թողնի էսպես,
Բոզալուկ ուլեր չարչարում են քեզ.
Էգուց նախիրը կը տանես արոտ։
Ասավ Օհանը ու միւս առավոտ
Գնաց, նորից նոր մեր Դավթի ոտի
Մի ջուխտ նոր տրեխ բերավ երկաթի,
Երկաթի մի կու հարիւր լիբրական
Ու չինեց Սասմայ քաղքի նախրապան։

VIII

Քշեց նախիրը մեր նախորդ հսկան,
Ելավ Սասունի սարերն աննման։
    —«Է'յ, ջան սարեր,
    Սասման սարե'ր,
    Ի'նչ անուշ է
    Ձեր լանջն ի վեր»...
Որ կանչեց, նրա ձենից ահալոր
Դղորդ-դղրդըմբրոցն ընկալ սար ու ձոր։
Վայրի գազաններ բներից փախան,
Քարեքար ընկան, դատարկուն եղան։
Դավիթն էր, ընկալ նրանց եւետից,
Որին մի սարից, որին մի ձորից,
Գայլ, ինձ, աոիւծ, արջ ու վագրը բռնեց,
Հալաքեց, բերալ, իր նախրին խառնեց
Ու առաջն արալ դէպ Սասմայ քաղաք։

"Take care, Uncle Ohan, tread softly,
Or else the goats will scamper off." And near by
An ash-colored hare, its ears fixed rigid,
Became frightened and bounded away.
David was quickly up and after it:
He trapped the hare in the hills, brought it back,
And placed it again among the goats.
"Oh, how hard it is, Uncle Ohan,
God has blessed the black goats, but these
Ash-colored goats are forever escaping
And scattering into the hills.
I raced so much and suffered so, yesterday,
Until I'd gathered them and brought them back."
Ohan saw that David's boots were not what
They had been, that his goatherd's staff had worn to the butt,
So much had he run in a single day.
"David, my soul, I cannot leave you like this,
Tortured so by the ash-colored goats.
Tomorrow take the flocks to pasture,"
Ohan said. And next morning he came back
Bringing still another pair of iron boots
For David's feet, and bringing an iron staff
A hundred pounds in weight, he made David
Pasture-keep of Sassountown.

VIII

The mighty shepherd drove his herd of cattle
And mounted Sassoun's peerless fastnesses.

> "O endearing highlands,
> Highlands of Sassoun,
> How sweetly the earth rises
> Against your rock-ribbed sides . . ."

When David sang, his voice had such force
That the canyons and highlands rang with it,
Wild animals sprang from their lairs, scattered
Over the rocks, and wandered homeless. David
Went after them all, those from the valleys,
Those from the hills—wolf, leopard, lion, bear, tiger,
He caught these,—gathered them and mixed them with his herd,
And at night drove them all down to Sassountown.

Ռունո՛ց, մռնչի՛ն, աղմո՛լկ, աղաղա՛կ...
Վախկոտ քաղցցիք մին էլ ի՛նչ տեսան,
Հէնց քաղքի վրայ անհամար գազան...

    — «Վա՛յ, Հարա՛յ, փախէ՛ք...»
    Մեծեր, երեխէք
    Սրտաճաք եղած,
    Գործները թողած

Փախան, ներս ընկան տուն, ժամ կամ խանութ,
Ամուր փակեցին դուռն ու լուսամուտ։
Դալիթը եկաւ կանգնեց մեյդանում.
—Վա՛հ, էս քաղցցիք ի՛նչ վաղ են քնում։

    Հէ՛յ կովատեր, հէ՛յ գոմշատեր,
    Ելէ՛ք, շուտով բացէ՛ք դռներ,
    Ով մի՛նն ունէր 'տա'ան եմ բերել։
    Ով տա՛ան ունէր — քսա'նն արբեր
    Շուտով ելէ՛ք, եկէ՛ք, տարէ՛ք,
    Ձեր եզն ու կով գոմերն արէք։

Տեսաւ՝ չեն գալի, դուռ չեն բաց անում,
Ինքն էլ մեկնուեց քաղքի մեյդանում,
Գլուխը դրաւ մի քարի, մնաց,
Ու մուշ-մուշ քնեց մինչեւ լուսաբաց։
Լուսին իշխաններ եկան միասին,
Գնացին Ձէնով Օհանին ասին․

—Ամա՛ն, քեզ մատաղ, ա՛յ Օհան ախպեր,
Մեր եզն ու մեր կով թող մնան անտեր,
Միայն սրանից ազա՛տ արա մեզ։
Ո՛չ արջն է ջոկում, ո՛չ գոմէշն ու եզ,
Մի օր էս քաղքին փորձանք կը բերի,
Արջերոց կ՚անի, կը տայ կ՚աւերի։

IX

Դալիթ չդառա՛լ, մի կրա՛կ դառալ։
Ճարը կտրրուած՝ Օհանը բերալ
Նետ-աղեղ չինեց ու տուալ իրեն՝
Գնայ, որս անի սարերի վրէն։
Դալիթ նետ-աղեղն առալ Օհանից,
Հեռացալ Սասմայ քաղքի սահմանից
Ու դառալ որսկան։ Գնաց, մի կորկում*
*Կարեկի արտ։

The noise, the commotion, the dust and the roar,
The charging of numberless beasts let loose:
This the townspeople suddenly heard and saw.

> "Oh! Help! Run!"
> Old and young,
> Panic-stricken,
> Ran away from their chores.

Some ran home, some to church, and some to shops;
All bolted their doors fast and closed the shutters tight.
David boldly entered and stood in the town square:
"Well, how early these people have gone to sleep!

> Ho there, oxen owners, cow owners,
> Get up swiftly, unbar your doors;
> He who had one, I've brought him ten,
> He who had ten, I've brought him scores.
> Up, get up swiftly, come and take them,
> Take your oxen and your cows to the barns."

When David saw that no one stirred, no one
Unbarred a door, he placed his head on
A stone, stretched himself out in the square,
And slept soundly until the break of day.
At dawn the burghers rose and together
Went to big-voiced Ohan and said,

"Big-voiced brother Ohan, alas, death take you,
It was you who brought up this fool and made him herdsman;
Let our cows and our oxen be unshepherded,
Let them be, but rid us of this foolish lout.
He does not part bears from ram or oxen;
Some day he'll bring great harm to our town,
He'll make it a bear's den, a forsaken land."

IX

Soon David changed; he became a firebrand.
Put to it, and driven to the end of his wits,
Ohan fashioned and gave to David
A bow and arrow. "Go forth and hunt among the hills."
David took from Ohan the bow and arrow,
And went beyond the boundaries of Sassoun;
He became a huntsman. Into a barley field

Լոր էր սպանում, ճնճղուկ էր զարկում,
Մթանը գնում իրեն հոր ծանոթ
Աղքատ, անորդի մի ձեր կնկայ մոտ,
Վիշապի նման, երկա՛ր, աճապի՛ն
Մեկնըլում՝ քնում կրակի կողքին։
Մեկնըլում, քնում կրակի կողքին։
Մի օր էլ, երբ որ իր որսից դարձալ,
Պառաւը վրէն սատիկ բարկացաւ.
— Վա՛յ Դալիթ, — ասաւ, — մահա տանի քեզ,
Դո՞ւ պէտք է էն հոր գաւակը լինե՛ս։
Ձեռից ու ոտից ընկած մի ձեր կին —
Ես եմ ու էն արտն Աստըծու տակին,
Ինչո՞ւ ես գնում, տափում, տրորում,
Իմ ամբողջ տարուան ապրուստը կորում։
Թէ որսկա՛ն ես դու — նետ աղեղըդ ա՛ռ,
Ծծմակայ գլխից մինչեւ Սեղանսար
Քուլ Հէրը ձեռին մի աշխարհ ունէր,
Որսով մէջը լի որսի սար ունէր.
Եղնի՛կ կայ էնտեղ, այծեա՛մ ու պախրա.
Կարո՞ղ ես — գնա՛, էնտե՛ղ որս արա։
— Ի՞նչ ես, ա՛յ պառաւ, էլ ի՞նչ անիծում.
Ես ջահել եմ դեռ, ես նոր եմ լսում։
Ո՞րտեղ է Հապա սարը մեր որսի...
— Գնա՛, հօրեղբայրդ — Օհանը կ՚ասի։

X

Հօրեղբօր չէմքում միս օրը ծեգին
Դալիթը կանգնեց աղեղը ձեռքին։
— Հօրեղբա՛յր Օհան, ինչո՞ւ չես ասել՝
Իմ Հէրը որսի սար է ունեցել,
Այժեամ կայ էնտեղ, եղջերու, կխտար։
Վե՛ր կաց, հօրեղբա՛յր, տա՛ր ինձ որսասար։
— Վա՛յ, — կանչեց Օհան, — էդ քուլ խոսքը չէր,
Էդ ո՞վ քեզ ասել, լեզո՛ւն պապանձէր։
Էն սարը, որդի՛, գնաց մեր ձեռից,
Էն սարի որսն էլ գնաց էն սարից,
Էլ չկան այժեամ, եղջերու, կխտար։
Քանի լուսեղէն քուլ Հէրը դեռ կար,
(Է՜յ դիտի օրեր — ո՛րտեղ էք կորել,)
Ես շատ եմ էնտեղ որսի միս կերել...

He sallied, killing quail, shooting sparrows,
And at dusk he took shelter in the hut
Of a poor and childless beldam
His father had once known. There, alongside
The fire, like an immense, long dragon,
He would stretch himself out and sleep.
One day, when he returned from the hunt,
The beldam raged at him. "Goodness, David!" she cried,
"Death take you! Are you indeed your father's son?
That field and I alone remain below
The skies and God. I am an old lady, weak
Of hand and foot—why do you trample
My field and lay it waste,
Why cut off my whole year's living? If you are
A huntsman, take up your bow and arrow—take
Yourself to the headlands of Zudsmaga, all
The way to Seghansar: your sire held there
The tenancy of an entire domain;
Its highlands are well-stocked with a game preserve;
There are deer there, mountain goats and wild sheep.
If you can, go, go and seek your game there."
"What is it, you hag, that makes you curse me?
I am still a stripling, I have heard only now.
Where, then, is the fastness of our game preserve?"
"Go to your uncle, Ohan will tell you."

X

Next day at sunrise David stood before
His uncle's threshold, bow in hand.
"Uncle Ohan, why haven't you told me
My father owned a mountain game preserve?
There are mountain goats there, rams and deer.
Up, uncle, bestir yourself and take me there."
"What!" cried Ohan, "These are not your words.
Whoever told it you, may his tongue be tied.
That mountain game preserve, my son, is lost
To us, as is the game of that range.
There are no more mountain goats, rams, and deer.
In the days when your father was still alive
(O what wondrous days, where have they fled?)
I often ate the flesh of game there . . .

Քու հէրը մեռաւ, Աստուած խոռվեց,
Մսրայ թագաւոր զօրքեր ժողովեց,
Եկաւ, մեր երկիր քարուքանդ արաւ,
Էս սարի ուրան էլ թալանեց, տարաւ.
Եղնիկը դնաց, եղջերուն դնաց...
Մեր գիրն էլ Հալբաթ էսպէ՞ս էր գրած։
Անցել է, օրդի, քու բանի՛ն դնա,
Մսրայ թագաւոր ճէնդ կ՚իմանայ...
—Մսրայ թագաւոր ինձ ի՞նչ կ՚անի որ...
Ես ի՞նչ եմ Հարցնում Մսրայ թագաւոր.
Մսրայ թագաւոր թող Սըսրը կենայ,
Իմ հօր սարերում ի՞նչ գործ ունի նա...
Վե՛ր կաց, հօրեղբա՛յր, նետ-աղեղըդ առ,
Կապարծդ կապի՛ր, դնա՛նք որսասար։
Ելաւ Օհանը ճարը կտըրուած,
Գնացին տեսան՝ էլ ի՛նչ որսասար.
Անտառը ջարդած, պարիսպն աւերած,
Բուրգերը արած գետնին հաւասար...

XI

Գիշերը հասաւ, մնացին էնտեղ։
Չէնով Օհաննն էր, իր նետոն ու աղեղ
Դրաւ գլխի տակ, Հանգիստ խորմփաց.
Դաւիթը մնաց մտքի ծովն ընկած։
Մին էլ ընկատեց, որ մութը հեռում՝
Մի թեժ, փայլփլուն կրակ է վառւում։
Էն լուսը բռնած՝
Վեր կացաւ, դնաց,
Գնաց ու դնա՛ց, բարձրացաւ մի սար,
Բարձրացաւ, տեսաւ մի մեծ մարմար քար
Կիսից պատռուած,
Ու միջից վառւած
Բխում է լուսը պա՛րզ, քուլայ-քուլա՛յ,
Բարձրանում, իջնում ետ քարի վրայ։
Վար իջաւ Դաւիթ էնտեղից կրկին,
Վար իջաւ, կանչեց Չէնով Օհանին.
—Է՛լ, հօրեղբա՛յր, քանի՛ քնես,
Է՛լ, էն պայծառ լուսը մի տես։
Լուս է իջել բարձըր սարին,
Բարձըր սարին, մարմար քարին։
Է՛լ, հօրեղբայր, անուշ քնից.
էն ի՞նչ լուս է բխում քարից։
Ելաւ, խաչ քաշեց Օհաննն երեսին.

Your father died, God forsook us, Egypt's king
Gathered soldiers, came upon us; he ruined
Our country, and this mountain game
He took, he plundered: the deer and the hind are gone.
So far has the scroll of our fate been written.
All is past, my son, go back to your work,
Lest the king of Egypt hear your voice."
"What can the king of Egypt do to me?
What do I ask from the king of Egypt?
Let the king of Egypt stay in Egypt;
What right has he to my father's highlands?
Get up uncle, take up your bow and arrow,
Buckle on your quiver, to the highlands
Let us go, to the mountain game preserve!"
Ohan stood, not knowing what to do.
But they went, and what a game preserve they saw—
The great walls demolished, the thick forests felled,
The high turrets smashed level with the earth.

XI

Night fell and they remained there. Big-voiced
Ohan placed beneath his head his quiver
And bow and snored peacefully. David
Was plunged into a sea of reckonings.
And soon he saw, in the dark distance,
A flaming strong fire burning brightly.
David moved toward the fire, and held by
Its spell, was quickly borne upon it;
Up and up he went, lighted on
A peak, ascended again, and saw a great
Cleft marble stone, belching from its center
Pure flame, rising and falling, tower
On tower, on the selfsame stone.
Now David descended, descended
And called big-voiced Ohan. "Up, uncle, up,
And see that bright fire, burning so brilliantly there.
How long are you going to sleep! A light has come down
From the steep hill, that steep marble stone hill.
Rise uncle, from your peaceful sleep. What light
Is that, that issues from that marble stone?"
Ohan stood and made the sign of the cross
Before his face. "Alas, my son," he said,
"How I idolize that light! That is the light

—Է՛յ, որդի, — ասաւ, — մեռնե՛մ իր լուսին,
էն մեր Մարութայ սարն է գօրաւոր։
էն լուսի տեղը կանգնած էր մի օր
Սասմայ ապալէն, Սասմայ պահապան
Մեր սուրբ Տիրամօր վանքը Զարխափան։
Աշտական, երբ որ կռիւ էր գնում,
էնտեղ էր քուլ Հէրն իր աղօթքն անում։
Քուլ Հէրը մեռաւ, Աստուած խոտվեց,
Մարայ թագաւոր գօրքեր ժողովեց,
Մեր վանքն էլ եկաւ քանդեց էն սարում,
Բայց դեռ սեղանից լուս է բարձրանում...

XII

Դաւիթը էս էլ երբ որ իմացաւ,
—Անո՛ւշ Հօրեղբայր, Հօրեղբրա՛յր, — ասաւ, —
Որբ եմ ու անտէր աշխարքի վրայ,
Հէր չունեմ՝ դու ինձ Հէրութին արա՛։
էլ չեմ իջնի ես Մարութայ սարից,
Մինչեւ չշինեմ մեր վանքը նորից։
Քեզանից կ՚ուզեմ հինգհարիւր վարպետ,
Հինգհազար բանուոր մշակ նրանց հետ,
Որ գան՝ էս շաբաթ կանգնեն ու բանեն,
Առաջուան կարգով մեր վանքը շինեն։
Գնաց Օհանը ու բերաւ իր հետ
Հինգ հազար բանուոր, հինգհարիւր վարպետ։
Վարպետ ու բանուոր եկան կանգնեցին,
Զըրը՛խկ, հա, Քըրը՛խկ, նորից շինեցին,
Առաջուան կարգով, փառքով փառաւոր՝
Բարձր Մարութայ վանքը Տիրամօր։
Յրուած միաբանք ետ նորից եկան,
Նորի՛ց թնդացին աղօթք, շարական.
Ու երբ չեն արաւ հօր վանքը նորից,
Յած իջաւ Դաւիթ Մարութայ սարից։

XIII

Համբաւը տարան Մսրայ Մելիքին.
—Հապա՛ չես ասի՝ Դաւիթը կրկին

From our great mountain, Marouta. In the place
Where that light stands once stood our Sassoun's
Patroness (what wondrous days!), Sassoun's guardian,
The Blessed Madonna's monastery
Of Charghopan. Always, when he went to war,
Your father made his prayers there.
Your father died, God became cross and was angry,
The king of Egypt gathered soldiers,
Marched on our abbey on that hill,
And levelled it—but from the altar, still,
The sacred flames of our patroness rise."

XII

When David heard this, too, he said, "Sweet uncle,"
"Sweet uncle, I am an orphan and liegeless
In this world. And lacking a father, I ask you
To be a father and good to me. I'll not again
Come down from Marouta's heights until
I have once again stepped into our abbey.
I ask from you five hundred artisans
And five thousand workers to work with them,
So that this very week they can come and build
Our former abbey as it once stood."
Now Ohan went forth and brought back with him
Five thousand workers and five hundred artisans
Who in sound and fury built again,
Much as before and overlaid with glories,
Our Blessed Mary's abbey at Marouta.
The scattered clergy once again came back,
And again the sound of canticle
And prayer echoed through the abbey's walls.
When his father's monastery was again
Full of people and merry, David then came down,
And only then he came down from Marouta's heights.

XIII

This news was taken to Melik of Egypt.
"Well, you don't say! So David has rebuilt

Հոր վանքը շինել, իշխան է դառել,
Դու օխտը տարուան խարջը չես առել։
Մելիք գայրացաւ․
—Գնացէ'ք, — ասաւ,
Բաղին, Կոզբաղին,
Սիւղին, Ջարխաղին,
Սասմայ քար ու հող տակն ու վե'ր արէք,
Իմ օխտը տարուան խարաջը բերէք։
Քառսուն կոյս աղջիկ բերէք արմաղան,
Քառսուն կարճ կնիկ, որ երկանք աղան,
Քառսուն էլ երկար, որ ուղտեր բառնան,
Իմ տանն ու դռան աղախին դառնան։
Ու Կոզբաղին առաւ գործեր․
—Գլխիս վրայ, — ասաւ, — իմ տէր, —
Գնամ Հիմի քանդեմ Սասուն,
Կանայք բերեմ քառսուն-քառսուն,
Քառսուն բեռնով դեղին ոսկի,
Տեղը չնչեմ Հայոց ազգի։
Ասաւ, Սարայ աղջիկ ու կին
Պար բռնեցին ու երգեցին․
—Մեր Կոզբաղին գնաց Սասուն,
Կանայք բերի քառսուն-քառսուն,
Քառսուն բեռնով ոսկի բերի,
Մեր ճակատին շարան շարի,
Կարմիր կովեր բերի կթան՝
Գառնան շինենք եղ ու խորթան։
Ջա'ն Կոզբաղին, քա'ջ Կոզբաղին,
Սասմայ Դաւիթն դարկեց դետին։
Ու Կոզբաղին փրքուած, ուռած,
—Շնորհակալ եմ, քոյրե'ր, — դռաց,
Մինչեւ գալըս դեռ համբերէ'ք,
էն ժամանա'կ պիտի պարէք․․․

XIV

Էսպէս երգով,
Ջօռով-զօրքով
Գող Կոզբաղին մտաւ Սասուն․
Օհան լսեց՝ կապուեց լեզուն։
Աղ ու հացով,
Լաց ու թացով
Առաջն ելաւ,
Խնդիրք արաւ.

His father's abbey and become the ruler,
While I still have seven years' tribute to
Collect!" Melik was now in a great rage.
"Go," he said, "Patin, Gouzpatin, Sitvin,
Charghatin, lay waste to Sassoun's earth and stones.
Bring back to me my seven years' rich tribute.
Bring me forty radiant Sassoun virgins,
Forty short women to turn the millstones,
And forty tall to load the camel trains,
All to be at my beck and call, my house slaves."
Gouzpatin marshalled his true soldiers.
"Gladly, my lord," he said, "so be it.
I go immediately to Sassoun, to lay
It bare, to bring back groups of forty women
And forty camel loads of yellow gold,
And ruin the home of the Armenian."
So he spoke. Egyptian maids and women
Danced together, and raised their voices in song.
"Our Gouzpatin has gone to Sassoun,
'Groups of forty women I have brought,
And forty saddlebags of gold;
Before my eyes, in serried order,
I have brought red milch cows . . .
We'll have butter to churn in the springtime,'
O Gouzpatin, brave Gouzpatin,
David is cast in the dust."
Now Gouzpatin, swollen with pride, roared out,
"I thank you, my sisters all, but be patient
Till I return—it's then that you should dance."

XIV

Thus with a song,
With soldiers strong,

Haughty Gouzpatin entered Sassoun;
When Ohan heard this he was suddenly tongue-tied.

With bread and salt,
With tears and cries,
He bowed his head
Before their spears
And prayed for mercy.

—Ի՞նչ որ կ՚ուզես՝ ա՛ռ, տա՛ր, ամա՛ն.
Վա՛րդ աղջիկներ, կանայք Սասման,
Դառը դատած դեղին ոսկին,
Միայն թէ գթա՛ մեր խեղճ ազգին,
Մի՛ կոտորիր, մի՛ տար մաշու,
Վերեւ՝ Աստուած, ներքեւը՝ դու...
Ասաւ, բերաւ շարան-շարան
Վարդ աղջիկներ, կանայք Սասման:
Ու Կոզբադին կանգնեց, ջոկեց,
Մաքագն առաւ, դուռը փակեց,
Քառսուն կոյս աղջիկ, սիրուն, արմաղան,
Քառսուն կարճ կնիկ, որ երկանք աղան,
Քառսուն էլ երկար, որ ուղտեր առնան,
Մսրայ Մելիքին դարալաշ դառնան:
Դէզ-դէզ կիտեց դեղին ոսկին.
Սեւ սուդ կալաւ Հայոց ազգին:

XV

Հէ՛յ, ո՞ւր ես, Դաւի՛թ, Հայոց պաշտպան,
Քարը պատռուի — դո՛ւրս արի մէյդան:
Քանդած Հօր վանքը որ շինեց նորից,
Ցած իջաւ Դաւիթ Մարութայ սարից,
Ժանգոտած, անկոթ մի շեղբիկ գտաւ,
Գնաց՝ պառաւի շաղգամը մտաւ:
Պառաւն էր. եկաւ՝ անէ՛ծք, աղաղա՛կ.
—Վա՛յ, խելա՛ռ Դաւիթ, շաղգամի տեղակ
Դու կրա՛կ ուտես, ցա՛ւ ուտես, — ասաւ, —
Քու աչքն աշխարքում մենակ ի՞նչ տեսաւ.
Կորեկլս արբիր գետնին Հալասար,
է՛ս էր մնացել ձմեռուան պաշար,
է՛ս էլ կտրում ես,
էլ ո՞նց ապրեմ ես:
Թէ կորիճ ես դու, աղեղդ ա՛ռ, գնա՛,
Քու Հօր աշխարքին տիրութիւն արա՛,
Քու Հօր գանձը կե՛ր.
Թողել ես անտէր,
Մսրայ Թագաւոր դրկել է՝ տանի:
—էլ ի՞նչ ես վրէս բարկանում, նանի՛.
էդ ի՞նչ ես ասում, ես չեմ Հասկանում,
Մսրայ Թագաւոր մեր ի՞նչն է տանում:
—Մսրայ Թագաւոր մեր ի՛նչն է տանում...

"Take what you wish, so be it; take
Our rosy girls, the women of Sassoun,
The yellow gold that's hard come by, take these,
Take these, but show mercy on our hapless people.
Do not cut us down nor do us to our death,
God is above, below are you," he said.
He brought scores of rose-hued girls
And women of Sassoun. Standing tall,
Gouzpatin gleaned; he lodged the likelier of them
Deep in the hayloft and then he locked the door:
Forty radiant, beautiful Sassoun virgins,
Forty short women to turn the millstones,
And forty tall to load the camel trains,
All to be house slaves of Egypt's Melik.
And from its treasure mounds of yellow gold . . .
A pall of mourning wrapped the Armenian people.

XV

O David, where are you, guardian of
The Armenian people, O let the rock be split open,
Only come out into the open!
Once David had repaired the abbey of
His fathers, he came down from Marouta's high peak;
He found a tarnished, handleless blade and stepped
Into the grandam's turnip field. The hag
Came out crying and cursing. "David, you fool,"
She said, "may you one day eat fire and pain
Instead of turnips. In this whole wide world
Can your eyes see only me and what is mine?
You've levelled my field to the ground, you have,
Only this remained of my winter store,
This you have wasted, too; how shall I live now?
If you are brave, take your bow, be gone,
Hold sway only over your father's domains,
Eat only from your father's treasures,
Which you have left unprotected so long
That Egypt's king has sent to have them packed off."
"Why are you so angry with me, grandam?
I know nothing of what you say.
What is it Egypt's king is taking from us?"
"The Egyptian king, my stupid David,

Մսրայ թագաւոր քու ա՛չքն է հանում,
Դանդալոշ Դաւիթ· դրբկել է հրկն,
Եկել են Սասմայ քաղաքի վրկն
Բաղին, Կոզբաղին,
Սիւղին, Ջարխաղին,
Թալան են տալի բովանդակ Սասում.
Քաոսուն բեռ ոսկի խարաջ են ուզում,
Քաոսուն կոյս աղջիկ սիրուն, արմաղան,
Քաոսուն կարճ կնիկ, որ երկանք աղան,
Քաոսուն էլ երկար, որ ուղտեր բառնան,
Մսրայ Մելիքին դարալաշ դառնան։
—Ի՞նչ ես, ա՛յ պաոաւ, էլ ինձ անիծում.
Յոյց տուր ինձ Հապա — ո՞րտեղ են ուզում։
—Ո՛րտեղ են ուզո՛ւմ... Մա՛հա տանի քե՛զ·
Դո՛ւ պէտք է էն Հօր պալակր լինե՛ս...
Եկել ես՝ չստեղ չազգամ ես լալում...
Ոսկին Կոզբաղին ձեր տանն է չափում,
Աղջիկներ փլեկ մարագն են լցրած։
Շաղգամը թողեց Դաւիթ ու գնաց։
Տեսաւ՝ Կոզբաղին իրենց տան միջին
Զափում է ոսկին թեղած առաջին,
Սիւղին, Ջարխաղին պարկերն են բռնել,
Չէնով Օհանն էլ չլինքը ծռեւ,
Կանգնել է Հեռու, ճեռները ծոցին։
Տեսաւ, աչքերը արևով լեցուեցին։
—Վե՛ր կաց, Կոզբաղին, Հեռո՛ւ կանգնիր դու,
Իմ Հօր ոսկին է — է՛ս եմ չափելու։
—Կոզբաղին ասաւ. — Է՛յ, Չէնով Օհան,
Կը տաս — տուր խարջը էս օրսոր տարուան,
Թէ չէ՝ կը գնամ, արեւս վկայ,
Մսրա-Մելիքին կը պատմեմ, կը գայ,
Ձեր Սասմայ երկիր քար ուքանդ կ՛անի,
Տեղը կը վարի, բոստան կը յանի։
—Կորէ՛ք, անգգամ դուք Մսրայ շներ,
Բա չէ՞ք իմացել դուք Սասմայ ծներ...
Մեռա՞ծ էք կարծում դուք մեզ, թէ՞ շուաք,
Կ՛ուզէք մեր երկիր դնէք խարջի տա՛կ...
Բարկացաւ Դաւիթ, չափը չպրտեց,
Տուաւ Կոզբաղնի գլուխը ջարդեց,
Զափի փշրանքը պատն անցաւ, գնաց,
Մինչեւ օրս էլ դեռ գնո՛ւմ է թռած։
Ու եղան՝ քափած ոսկին թողեցին,

Is gouging out your eyes: already
He is here. To the town of Sassoun have come Patin,
Gouzpatin, Sitvin, Charghatin; the whole
Of Sassoun they plunder, even now:
Forty saddlebags of gold for tribute,
Forty radiant, beautiful virgins,
Forty short women to turn the millstones,
Forty tall to load the camel trains,
All to be slaves to Egypt's king."
"O grandam, why do you curse me? Just show me,
Let me see—these demands, where are they made?"
"Death take you, David! Where are they made!
Are you really the son of that father,
You, who come here to munch on turnips?
In your own house Gouzpatin measures
Out your gold, while the pretty girls
Are locked together in your hayloft."
David left off eating turnips. He went,
Spied Gouzpatin in his house, counting
The gold spilled out before him while Charghatin
And Sitvin held the barking dogs;
At a distance, his neck bent to one side,
Ohan stood, arms folded across his breast.
David saw all this and his eyes gorged with blood.
"Stop! Gouzpatin, stand apart. My father's
Gold this is. I'm the one to count it out."
Gouzpatin said, "Well, big-voiced Ohan,
Will you give us this seven years' tribute, or not?
If not, may my whiskers be witness, I'll leave
And tell Musra-Melik, and he will come;
He'll waste your Sassoun's countryside,
Burn it down and plant a garden on it."
"Be gone, you unfeeling Egyptian dogs.
Have you not yet heard of Sassoun's reckless brave ones?
Do you think we all are dead, or merely shadows?
You think to place our country under tribute!"
David's anger was great. He snatched up and threw
The weighing scales, which smashed Gouzpatin's head—
Their fragments flew out beyond the walls, and till now,
To this very day, they are still in flight.
Now the Egyptians rose, let be the scattered gold,

Հայոց աշխարքից փախան գնացին
Բաղին, Կողբադին,
Սիւդին, Զարխադին։

XVI

—Վա՛յ, վա՛յ, Հօրեղբա՛յր, ի՞նչ ասեմ ես քեզ.
Մենք ունենք չստեղ դեղին ոսկու դէզ,
Դու արել ես ինձ քաղաքի ծառան,
Դու թողել ես ինձ օտարի դռան...
Հօրեղբայրն ասաւ.— Ա՜յ խենթ, խելագար,
Ոսկին պահել եմ Մելիքի համար,
Որ քաղցըր լինի աչքը մեզ վրայ։
Ջրտուիր, Հիմի որ գործք առնի՝ գայ,
Սասմայ քար ու հող Հեղեղի՛, տանի՛,
Ո՞վ դէմը կ՚երթայ, ո՞վ կռիւ կ՚անի։
—Դու կա՛ց, Հօրեղբա՛ր, թող գայ, ե՛ս կ՚երթամ,
Կ՚երթամ, ե՛ս նրան պատասխան կը տամ։
Ու մութ մարագի դռանը գարկեց,
Փակած աղչիկներ Հանեց, արձակեց։
—Գնացէ՛ք,— ասաւ,— ազատ ապրեցէ՛ք,
Սասունցի Դաւթին արեւ խնդրեցէք։

XVII

Էսպէս չարդուած, արիւնլուայ
Փախան, ընկան Հօղը Մսրայ
Բաղին, Կողբադին,
Սիւդին, Զարխադին։
Մսրայ կանայք Հեռուից տեսան,
Հեռուից տեսան, ուրախացան
Ու ծափ տուին կոտերերին

—Եկա՛ն, եկա՛ն, բերի՛ն, բերի՛ն...
    Մեր Կողբադին գնաց Սասուն,
    Կանայք բերաւ քարսուն-քարսուն,
    Կարմիր կովեր բերաւ կթան՝
    Գարնան չինենք եղ ու չորթան...
Հէնց մօտեցան, նկատեցին,
Ծափ ու խնդում ընդհատեցին
Քրքշացին
Ու կանչեցին.
—Է՛յ, Կողբադին մեծաբերան,
Էդ ո՞րտեղից լերան-լերան,

Left far behind the Armenian world and fled,
Patin, Gouzpatin, Sitvin, Charghatin.

XVI

"Well, well, what shall I say to you, uncle?
We have here mounds and mounds of gold.
You've made of me a servant of the town,
And abandoned me before an alien's door."
"You crazy fool," his uncle said, "I've kept
All this gold for Melik that he might kindly
Look upon us. Now that you will not give it,
Who is there who will face his wrath, fight him
When he comes with his soldiers and with fire
To lay Sassoun's earth and stones in ruins?"
"Stay, uncle, let him come; I shall go,
I shall go and make an answer to him."
He shattered the door of the darkened hayloft,
Let out the pinioned girls, and set them free.
"Go," he said, "live in freedom, and do not fail
To pray long days for David of Sassoun."

XVII

So, slaughtered in this way and bathed in blood,
They fled homeward and reached their native land,
Patin, Gouzpatin,
Sitvin, Charghatin.
Egyptian women saw them in the distance,
Saw them in the distance and were glad—
From the rooftops the women clapped and cheered them home.

> "They're coming, they're coming . . .
>   they bear, they bear . . .
> Our Gouzpatin has come from Sassountown,
> He's brought back groups of forty women, red milch cows,
> In the spring we'll butter make and chortaan."

But once they saw
At closer range
That Gouzpatin was bloodied,
They ceased their giggling

Chortaan is a light, yogurt-based beverage.

Լերան-լերան կը դաս փախած,
Հաստ դլուխդ կիսից ճղած։
Էն դու չասի°ր՝ դնամ Սասուն,
Կանայք բերեմ քառսուն-քառսուն,
Քառսուն բեռնով ոսկի հանեմ,
Հայոց երկիր ալեր անեմ։
Գացիր Սասուն քանց գել գազան,
Եու ես դալի քանց չո՛լն վազան...
Ու Կողբադին խիստ բարկացալ.
—Մո՛լս կացէք դուք, լրբե՛ր, — ասալ.
Ձեր մարդիկն էք տեսել դուք դեռ,
Դուք չէք տեսել Սասմայ ծռեր։
Սասմայ ծռեր լերան-լերան,
Նետեր ունեն մի-մի գերան.
Սասմայ երկիր քար ու կապան,
Դժար սարեր, ձոր ու ծապան.
Նրանց խոտեր — ինչպէս կեռ թութր,
Զորք ջարդեցին երեք հարիւր...
Ասաւ ու էլ չառաւ դադար,
Վռազ-վռազ, գլխապատառ
Վազեց իրեն թագաւորին։
Խնդաց թագլորն իր աթոռին։
—Ապրե՛ս, ապրե՛ս, քաջ Կողբադին,
Արժէ՝ կախեմ ես քու ճտին
Մեր դուզզունի* մեծ նշանը —
Պարգեւ քու մեծ յաղթութեանը։
Սասմայ ոսկին ու աղջիկներ։
Ասաւ Մելիք, ու Կողբադին
Գլուխ տուաւ մինչեւ գետին։
—Ապրա՛ծ կենաս, մեծ թագաւոր,
Զօռով փախայ ես ճիալոր,
Ո°նց բերէի Սասմայ ոսկին։
Մի խենթ ծնուեց Հայոց ազգին,
Ո'չ աճ գիտի, ո'չ տէր ու մեծ,
Գլուխս էսպէս տուաւ, ջարդեց.
«Զե՛մ տալ, — ասաւ, — իմ հօր ոսկին,
Զե՛մ տալ կանայքն իմ հայ ազգին,
Սասմայ երկիր ձեզ տեղ չկա՛յ...
Քու թագաւոր, — ասաւ, — թո՛ղ գայ,
Թող գայ՝ ինձ հետ կռիւ անի,
Թէ դուչաղ է՝ գօռով տանի»։
Կատաղեց, փրփրեց Մսրայ թագաւոր.
—Կանչեցնէ՛ք, — ասաւ, — իմ գօրքը բոլոր.

And taunted him.
"Well, Gouzpatin, you loud-mouthed coward,
Down what slopes and over what mountains have you fled,
With your thick head cut in half? Didn't you say
'I go to Sassoun to bring back groups of forty women
And forty saddlebags of yellow gold,
And lay waste the country of the Armenians'?
As a panting, fleeing hound you have returned!"
Now horribly angered, Gouzpatin began to speak:
"Silence, you brats, you've seen only your own breed
Of men and not the reckless, brave men of Sassoun.
Sassoun's fearless braves are like mountains,
Their arrows thick as stakes, and their country,
To top it all, a stony fastness: canyon walls—
Impenetrable—abound, and steep-sided hollows;
Even their blades of grass are curved as swords . . .
They slaughtered three hundred men, the best in Egypt."
So he spoke and once he had, he didn't stay,
But ran fast, head over heels and pell-mell,
Ran right up to the king. The king laughed from
His throne. "Live, O live, brave Gouzpatin.
The famed medallion of Ghouzghoun, richly
Do you deserve it, and it shall hang from your neck,
As reward for your great and sweeping triumph.
But where are they? Bring me Sassoun's girls and gold."
Thus Melik spoke, but Gouzpatin had bowed
His head to the very ground. He said,
"Live long, O great king! I could hardly escape,
Though mounted on my horse. How could I
Have taken Sassoun's yellow gold? A fool has been
Born to the Armenians, one who will bear with nor
Lord nor fear nor mighty men. See how he's
Bloodied my head and smashed it!
'I will not give my father's gold,' he said,
'Nor will I give the women of my
Armenian people. In the country of Sassoun
There is no room for you. Your king,' he said,
'Let him come, let him come and fight with me.
If he is brave, let him come and take by force.' "
The enraged Egyptian king flamed out.
"Call all my soldiers together," he said, "call

Հազար հազար մարդ նորելուկ մանուկ,
Հազար հազար մարդ անբեխ, անմօրուք,
Հազար հազար մարդ բեխը նոր ձլած,
Հազար հազար մարդ նոր թախտից ելած,
Հազար հազար մարդ թուխ միրուքալոր,
Հազար հազար մարդ սիպտակ ալեւոր,
Հազար հազար մարդ, որ փողեր հնչեն,
Հազար հազար մարդ, որ թմբուկ զարկեն...
Կանչեցէ՛ք, թող գան, հազնեն գէ՛նք, գրա՛ն,
Կռիւ տի գնամ ես Դալթի վրայ,
Սասունն ալերե՛մ,
Հեղեղե՛մ, բերե՛մ։

XVIII

Էսպէս անհամար գորքեր հաւաքեց,
Եկաւ Սասմայ դաշտ, բանակը զարկեց
Ու ձանքը նստեց Մսրայ թագաւոր։
Էնքան աչագին բազմութիւնն էն օր
Բաթմանայ ջրին եկաւ ու չոքեց,
Ո՛վ եկաւ, խմեց — գետը ցամաքեց,
Սասմայ քաղաքում մնացին ճարալ։
Չէնով Օհանին գարմանքը տարաւ։
Քուրքը ուսն առաւ, սարը բարձրացաւ.
Սարը բարձրացաւ, տեսաւ, ի՞նչ տեսաւ։
Ճերմակ վրանից դաշտը ճերմակել,
Ասես՝ էն գիշեր ձմեռը եկել,
Սպիտակ ձիւնով պատել էր Սասուն։
Լեղին ջուր կտրեց, կապ ընկալ լեզուն,
Հարա՛յ կանչելով՝ փախաւ, տուն ընկաւ.
—Վա՛յ, փախէ՛ք, եկա՛ւ... հա՛յ, հարա՛յ, եկաւ...
—Ի՞նչը, հօրեղբա՛յր, ի՞նչը, ի՞նչն եկաւ...
—Ցայն ու կրա՛կը Դալթի պինչն եկաւ։
Մսրայ թագաւոր եկել է, եկել,
Եկել, մեր դաշտին բանակ է զարկել.
Թիւ կայ աստղերին, թիւ չկայ գորքին...
Վա՛յ մեր արեւին, վա՛յ մեր աշխարքին...
Ե՛կ, ոսկին տանենք, աղջիկներ տանենք,
Ջոքենք առաջին, պաղատանք անենք,
Գուցէ թէ գթա՛յ,
Մեզ սրի չտա՛յ...
—Դու կա՛ց, հօրեղբա՛յր, դու դարդ մի՛ անիր.
Գնա՛, քու օղում դու հանգիստ քնիր։
Հիմի ես կ՚ելնեմ, Սասմայ դաշտ կ՚երթամ,

A thousand thousand males, newborn infants,
A thousand thousand males without beards or moustaches,
A thousand thousand males with downy lips,
A thousand thousand males fresh from couches,
A thousand thousand males with black moustaches,
A thousand thousand males whose hair is grey,
A thousand thousand males to sound the trumpets,
A thousand thousand males to strike the war drums—
Have them come forth, and take up arms and armor:
I go to wage war on David, destroy
Sassoun, and plunder it to the ground."

XVIII

So he assembled an innumerable
Host, marched on the plains of Sassoun and encamped there
In full solemnity, this Egyptian king.
Their number was so great
That when they came to Batman's banks, bent down
And drank their fill, they drank the river dry
And Sassoun's townsfolk were parched with thirst.
Big-voiced Ohan was surprised.
An animal skin on his shoulders, he climbed to the heights,
He climbed to the heights, and O, what met his eyes:
The bleached tents had so whitened the plains
It seemed that a midwinter night had come
And covered Sassoun with deep white snow.
His gall turned to water, his tongue was tied,
And then shouting halloo he rushed back home.
"Halloo, run, it's come—holla, soho, it's come—"
"What, uncle, what? What has come, who?"
Horrid fire and pain now came to David's nose.
"Egypt's king has risen and come, come and filled
Our plain with his tented armies. The stars
May be numbered but not this numberless host.
Alas, for our lives, alas, for our world!
Come, let's take the gold, let's take the girls,
Let's fall to the ground before him and say prayers;
Perhaps he'll relent and forbear to use the sword."
"Stay, uncle, don't be afraid; go to
Your quiet room and sleep there peacefully.
But I'll get up now, go to Sassoun's plain,

Մարա-Մելիքին պատասխան կը տամ։
Ու գնաց Դաւիթ ծանօթ պառաւին.
—Նանի քա՛ն, — ասաւ, — ժանգոտած ու հին
Երկաթի կտոր, անթարող, չամփուր,
Ինչ ունե՛ս չունես՝ հաւաքի՛ր, ինձ տուր,
Մի էշ էլ գտիր, որ վրէն նստեմ,
Կեի՛լ տի գնամ Մսրայ գործի դէմ։
—Վա՛յ, Դաւիթ, — ասաւ, — մա՛հա տանի քեզ.
Դո՞ւ պէտք է էն հօր գալակը լինե՛ս...
Քու Հերն ունէր կռուի համար
Հրեղէն ձի, ոսկի քամար,
Ջրած չապիկ, կապէն հագի,
Աջ թեւին խաչ պատարագի,
Կուռ սադաւարտ, Կայծակի-Թուր,
Իսկ դու կ'ուզես էշ ու չամփո՞ւր...
—Ամա՛ն, նանի՛, չեմ լսել դեռ.
Ո՛րը են հիմի իմ հօր գէնքեր։
—Հօրեղբօ՛րդ գնա, հարցո՛ւր.
Ո՞րը են, ասա, հանի՛ր, բե՛ր, տո՛ւր։
Բան է, թէ որ չտայ սիրո՛վ,
Ա՛շքը հանիր՝ խլիր գօռո՛վ։

XIX

Դաւիթ գնաց հօրեղբօր մօտ.
—Է՛յ հօրեղբայր, — կանչեց Հերսոտ,
Իմ Հէրն ունէր կռուի համար
Հրեղէն ձի, ոսկի քամար,
Ջրած չապիկ, կապէն հագի,
Աջ թեւին խաչ պատարագի,
Կուռ սադաւարտ, Կայծակի-Թուր.
  Կը տաս՝ բե՛ր, տո՛ւր...
  —Վա՛յ, Դաւիթ ջա՛ն, —
Ահից գոռաց Ջէնով Օհան. —
Քու հօր մահուան տարուց — օրից
Դուրս չեմ հանել ձին ախոռից,
Ոչ սնդուկից Թուր-Կայծակին,
Ջրած չապիկ, ոսկի գօտին...
Ինձ թող, ամա՛ն, մի՛ սպանիր,
Կ'ուզես — հրէն, գնա՛, հանի՛ր։

XX

Հագաւ Դաւիթ գէնքն ու գրած,
Կապեց գօտին, Թուր-Կայծակին,

And make my answer to Egypt's king."
David then went straight to his trusted grandam.
"Granny, my soul," he said, "give me some scraps
Of iron, old and tarnished, a grate, a spit—
Gather whatever you can and give it to me;
Also find me an ass on which I may ride.
I go to war against the Egyptian host."
"My goodness, David," she said, "death take you!
Can you indeed be the son of your father?
In war your father rode a fiery steed,
Fully caparisoned, with a bellyband of gold;
He had a steel club, a pearled saddle, a hardy helmet,
And on his right arm a ready cross,
A mailed vest, and a sword fashioned from lightning.
And now you have come here, you silly, madcap fool,
Asking from me an ass and an old spit."
"O granny, I never heard of these things before.
Where is my father's armor now?"
"Go to your uncle now, ask him,
Say 'Where are they? Find them, bring them, give them to me'.
If he does not willingly give them to you,
Gouge out his eyes," she said, "and take them forcibly."

XIX

And David went to see his uncle Ohan.
"O uncle," he called angrily, "for battle
My father had a fiery steed, fully
Caparisoned, with a bellyband of gold;
He had a steel club, a pearled saddle, a hardy helmet,
And on his right arm a ready cross,
A mailed vest, and a sword fashioned from lightning."
"O David, my soul," Ohan roared in fear,
"Since the day of your father's death
I have not brought the steed from the barn,
Nor the sword of lightning from the arms chest,
Nor the mailed vest, the golden bellyband. . . .
For goodness sake, let me be, plague me not,
If you want these scamper off and get them."

XX

David clapped on his armor and his mail,
Buckled, too, the belt of his lightning sword

Խաչն էլ իր յաղթ բագևի վրայ,
Ելաւ, հեծաւ Աուիծ հօր ճին,
Հօր ճին հեծաւ ու մտրակեց․
Չէնով Օհան լայով երգեց․
— Ափսո՛ս, հազա՛ր ափսոս Հրեղէն մեր ճին,
   Ա՛խ, Հրեղէն մեր ճին․
Ափսո՛ս, հազա՛ր ափսոս մեր ոսկի գոտին,
   Ա՛խ, մեր ոսկի գոտին․
Ափսո՛ս, թանկ կապէն, որ Հագին տարաւ,
   Ա՛խ, որ Հագի՛ն տարաւ․․․

   Դաւիթ բարկացաւ,
   Չին քշեց, դարձաւ,
   Օհանը վախեց,
   Իր երգը փոխեց․
«Ափսո՛ս, նորեւուկ Դաւիթս կորաւ,
   Ա՛խ, Դաւիթս կորաւ։»
Էս որ իմացաւ,
Դաւիթ մեղմացաւ,
Իջաւ, Օհանի ճեռքը համբուրեց։
Չէնով Օհանն էլ, ինչպէս Հայր ու մեծ,
Օրհնեց, խրատեց նրան Հայրաբար,
Դէպի Սասմայ դաշտ դրաւ ճանապարհ։

XXI

Սասունցի Դաւիթն ունէր մի քեռի,
Անունը Թորոս, ահեղ աժդահայ։
Սա էլ իմացաւ համբաւը կռուի,
Մի բարդի ուսին գալիս է ահա։
Գալիս է՝ Հեռուից բարձըր գոռալով․
— Ի՞նչ էք վեր եկել էս դաշտի միջում,
Քանի՞ գլխանի մարդիկ էք կամ ո՞վ,
Սասունցի Դաւթին որ չէ՛ք ճանաչում․․․
Բա՛, չէ՛ք իմանում, որ խստեղ է նա
Գալու՝ խաղացնի իր ճին թեւաւոր․
Չքուեցէ՛ք, հիմի ուր որ է՛ կը գայ,
Եկել եմ սրբեմ մէջդանը խսօր։

Ասաւ ուքաշեց իր ուսի բարդին,
Սրբեց բանակից մի քսան վրան․․․
Դաւիթն էլ ահա սարի գագաթին
Կանգնած՝ գոռում է վիշապի նման․

And, with the cross on his all-conquering arm,
Mounted his lion-hearted father's steed,
Mounted his father's steed and lashed it forward.
Big-voiced Ohan wept, and sang,
"Mercy, a thousand mercies
For this steed,
Alas, this fiery steed,
Mercy, a thousand mercies
For this bellyband,
Alas, this bellyband of gold,
Mercy that this rich array is lost,
Alas, that this rich array is lost."
David flew into a rage,
Turned his horse and drove it back;
Poor Ohan paled, stood still in fear,
And changed the tune of his song.
"Alas, my infant David's lost,
Alas, my David's lost . . . "
When David heard this
His temper cooled,
He dismounted and kissed Ohan's hand;
And as a father should, big-voiced Ohan
Blessed him, gave him paternal counsel,
And put him on the road to Sassoun plain.

XXI

Now David of Sassoun had an uncle—
Toros by name—a fearsome, giant-like man.
When he, too, heard the rumors of war,
He strode forth with an elm on his shoulder.
He approaches from a distance, roaring.
"Why have you come onto this field? Who are you,
How many soldiers are there among you?
Do you not know of David of Sassoun?
But haven't you heard he's on his way here,
And brings his winged horse to pace him around?
Clear away, David will be coming,
Wherever he is, I've come to make a clearing."

As he spoke, he brought the elm tree down
From his shoulder and swept away some twenty
Pitched tents of the army; David meanwhile stood

—Ո՛վ քնած էք՝ արթո՛ւն կացէք,
Ով արթուն էք՝ ելէ՛ք, կեցէ՛ք,
Ով կեցել էք՝ դէ՛նք կապեցէք,
Չէնք էք կապել՝ ձի՛ թամբեցէք,
Ձի էք թամբել՝ ելէ՛ք, հեծէ՛ք.
Ցեյոյ չասէք՝ թէ մենք քնած —
Դալիթ գող-գող եկաւ, գնա՛ց...
Էսպէս կանչեց, ասպանդակեց,
Ու, ինչ ամպից կայծակ գարկի,
Մարայ գօրքի մէջ տեղ-գարկեց,
Շողացնելով Թուր-Կայծակին:

Ձարդեց, փշրեց մինչեւ կէսօր.
Կէսօր արինն ելաւ Հեղեղ,
Քշեց, տարաւ Հագարաւոր
Մարդ ու դիակ ողջ միատեղ:

Կար գօրքի մէջ մի ալեւոր,
Աշխարք տեսած ու բանագէտ.
—Տղե՛րք, — ասաւ, — ճամբայ տուէք,
Գնամ խոսեմ ես Դալիթի Հետ:

Գնաց՝ կանգնեց Դալիթի առաջ,
Էսպէս խոսեց էն ծերունին.
—Դալար կենայ կոլորդ, ո՛վ քաջ,
Սուրդ կորուկ միշտ քու ճեռին:
Մի ծերունուս խօսքին մտիկ,
Տե՛ս, քու խելքը ինչ է կորում:
Ի՞նչ են արել քեզ էս մարդիկ,
Հէ՞ր ես սրանց դու կոտորում:
Ամէն մինը մի մոր որդի,
Ամէն մինը մի տան ճրագ,
Որբ կինն է թողել էնտեղ
Աչքը ճամբին, խեղճ ու կրակ,
Որբ մի տուն լիք մանուկներ,
Որբ ծնող աղքա՛տ ու ծեր,
Որբ լացով, քօղն երեսին
Նորապսակ ջահիլ Հարսին...
Թագաւորը գռով-թռով
Հաւաքել է, էստեղ բերել:

On a fearsome height and roared a dragon's roar.
"You who are asleep, wake up,
You who are awake, stand and attend,
You who are on foot, take up your arms,
You who are armed, saddle your horses,
You who are saddled, mount your horses—
That you may not say later that while you slept
David crept stealthily upon you and left."

Thus he roared, and goading his fiery steed,
Came down upon them like a lightning bolt from a cloud,
Spreading terror among the Egyptian armies,
Brandishing his lightning sword on all sides.

He smashed, slew, slaughtered till high noon,
At high noon the blood rose like a floodtide;
He herded up and drove off together
Thousands of the quick, among those dead.

Among the soldiers was an ancient man,
A sage, and one well-traveled in the world;
"Men," he said, "make way, make way for me,
I must go to David, must speak with him."

He went to David and stood before him;
And this is how the elder spoke:
"O brave one, may your fist ever stay strong,
And the short sword always in your hand.

But listen to the words of an old man
And see if there is any sense to them.
Pray tell me, what have these men done to you
That you drive on pell-mell to slaughter them?

Each one among them is a mother's son,
Each one a light burning in his home,
Far behind some have left their wives forlorn,
Wives who look to the road for their return.

Some have left homes filled with many children,
Some have left poor and aging parents,
And some have left, in tears, with their faces veiled,
The young brides of only yesterday . . .

Under the sway of the sword and by might, their king has
Gathered them and marched them here together.

Խեղճ մարդիկ ենք՝ պակաս օրով,
Մենք քեզ վնաս ի՞նչ ենք արել։
Թագավորն է քո թշնամին,
Կռի՛վ ունես — ի՛ր հետ արա,
Հէ՞ր ես քաշում Թուր-Կայծակին
Ես անճարակ խալխի վրայ։

—Լավ ես ասում դու, ձերունի՛, —
Ասաւ Դավիթն ալելորին,
Բայց Թագավորն ո՞ւր է հիմի,
Որ սել կապեմ նրա օրին։

—Մեծ վրանում քնած է նա,
Է՛ն, որ միջից ծուխը կ՚ելնի.
էն ծուխն էլ, Հօ՛, ծուխ չի՛ որ կայ,
Գոլորշին է իր բերանի։

Ասին. դեպի մեծ վրանը
Ասպանդակեց Դավիթն իր ձին,
Քշեց, գնաց ու դռանը
Գոռաց կանգնած արաքներին.

—Ո՞ւր է, — ասաւ, — ինչ է կորել,
Դո՛ւրս կանչեցէ՛ք, դայ ասպարէզ,
Թէ մաչ չունի՝ մա՛չ եմ բերել,
Գրո՛դ չունի՝ գրո՛դն եմ ես...

—Մելիքն, — ասին, — քուն է մտել,
Օխսր օրով պէտք է քնի.
Երեք օրն է դեռ անցկացել,
Չորս օր էլ կայ, քունը առնի։

—Ի՛նչ, բերել է աղքատ ու խեղճ
Խալխին լցրել ծովն արիւնի,
Ինքը մտել վրանի մէջ՝
Օխսր օրով հանգիստ քնի՛...
Քնել–մնել չեմ հասկանում,
Վե՛ր կացրէք չո՛լտ, դուրս դայ մէյդան,
Էնպէս դրան ես քնացնեմ,
Որ չզարթնի՝ էլ յաւիտեան։

Եղան՝ մարդիկ ճարահատած
Շամխուր դրին թէժ կրակին

We are men to be pitied, with hastening days,
What harm have we brought you, in what way?

Your enemy is the warring king, the king himself.
Go fight with him instead, if you must fight.
Pray sheath your lightning-laden sword,
Spare these helpless, unprotected people."

"You speak well and very true, old man,"
David said to the elder. "But where is the
Warring king? What is he doing now?
Let him show himself that I may wreathe his days in black."

"He has set out from the great tent, the one
That has the smoke issuing from its center;
That is not firesmoke you see rising to the sky,
It is smoke from the king's own fuming mouth."

Thus they spoke. Now David goaded his
Horse and rode straight to where the great tent stood.
He rode and rode up to the entrance door,
And thus he roared at the Arabs standing there:

"Where is he? Why has he become so scarce?" he said.
"Call him out, call him out into the open;
If he does not know death, I have brought him death,
If he does not know Sassoun's avenger, he am I."

"Melik," they said, "has gone to sleep. For days,
For seven days he must sleep. Only three days
Have passed yet, four more days
Remain before he will have had his share of sleep."

"What! Has he brought these poor pitiful folk,
Dumped them on this field, spilled their blood in seas,
While he finds shelter under cover of
His great tent and sleeps in peace for seven days!

I can not wait, whether he sleeps or not,
Quick! Get him up and into the open;
I'll put him to sleep, in such a way, before
His entrance door, he'll never wake again."

The men, taken aback, rose and spat on
The great burning fire; they tapped on

Ու գարկեցին խոր մրափած
Մարա-Մելքի բաց կրընկին։

—Օ՛ֆ, էլ հանգիստ քուն չունի մարդ
էս անիծուած լուի ճեղից, —
Խոր մունջաց հական հանդարտ
Ու չուր եկաւ, քնեց նորից։

Ելան, բերին մեծ գութանի
խոփը՝ դրին թեժ կրակին,
Ու կաս-կարմիր, կեծկըծալի,
Շիկնած տուին մերկ թիկունքին։

—Օ՛ֆ, էլ հանգիստ քուն չունի մարդ
էս անիրաւ մոծակներից. —
Աչքը բացաւ հական հանդարտ,
Ուզում էր ետ քնել նորից,
Տեսաւ՝ Դալթին։ Գլուխն ահեղ

Վեր բարձրացրեց մունջալով,
Փչեց վրէն, որ թոցընի
էն աժդըհին մի փչելով։

Տեսաւ, տեղից ժաժ չի գալի,
Զարմանքն ու ահ պատեց հոգին։
Արնոտ աչքերն ըսպառնալի
Յառեց խոժոռ Դալթի աչքին։

Նայեց թէ չէ, զգաց՝ իր մէջ
Տապը գոմշի ուժ պակասեց։
Պառկած տեղից վրայ նստեց
Ու ժպտակով հետը խօսեց։

—Բարո՛վ, Դալի՛թ, յօդնած ես դեռ.
Ե՛կ, մի նստի՛ր, խօսենք կարգին,
Ցեսոյ դարձեալ կռիւ կ՚անենք,
Եթէ կռիւ կ՚ուզես կրկին...

Իր վրանում բունակալը
Քաղսուն գաց խոր հոր էր փորել,
Ցանցով փակել մութ բերանը,
Վրէն փափուկ խալի փռել։
Ում որ յաղթել չէր կարենում,

The heels of the Egyptian king,
Who was sunk in a deep, peaceful sleep.

"How now! A body can no longer get
Peaceful sleep, the fleas are so annoying."
So the great burly king mumbled to himself,
Turned over, and once more fell fast asleep.

They left and returned with a huge plow;
They placed its share in the great, burning fire,
And when it was red-hot, reddened and sparkling,
They clapped it straightaway on his naked back.

"How now! A body can no longer get
Peaceful sleep, the mosquitoes are so cruel."
Slowly, the great burly king opened his eyes,
He wanted so to fall back to sleep.

But he saw David. Muttering to himself,
He lifted his enormous head from where he slept.
He blew a great blast of air on David,
Thinking it would set the giant to flight.

And when he saw that David stood stock still,
Surprise and dread struck his very soul.
He cast his menacing, bloodshot eyes sidelong,
Gloweringly at David's unblinking eyes.

But just as soon as he had looked, he felt
The strength of ten oxen had ebbed from him.
So on the place he had slept he now sat up
And, smiling, began to speak with David.

"Hello, David, well-met. You are still tired;
Come, sit down a bit—let's talk, as is proper,
Later we may still engage in battle,
That is, if you seek another battle . . ."

The scheming tyrant had within his great tent
Caused forty spans of deep wells to be dug,
The black mouths of which had been covered over
With screens, and over those some small, bright rugs.

It was always his practice to fawn on and lure
To him all those he failed to vanquish;

Շողումելով կանչում էր նա,
Նստեցնում էր իր վրանում
էն կորստեան հորի վրայ։

Իջաւ Դաւիթ ճիուղը ցած,
Գնաց, նստեց... ընկալաւՀորբ։
— Հա՛, հա՛, հա՛, հա՛, քահ-քահ խնդաց
Մարան դաժան թագաւորբ։

— Դէ՛, թող հիմի գնա՛յ,՝ խաւար
Հորում փթի, էնքան մնայ—։
Ու աՀագին մի ջաղացքար
Բերաւ, դրաւ հորի վրայ։

XXII

Քնեց էն գիշեր Չէնով Օհանբ։
Գիշերն երազում երեւաց ծերին՝
Մարայ երկնքում արեւ ճառագած,
Սեւ ամպ էր պատել Սասմայ սարերին։

Սաստիկ վախեցած վեր թռաւ տեղից։
— Վա՛յ, կնի՛կ, — ասաւ, — մի ճրագ արա՛,
Գնա՛ց մեր անխորճ Դաւիթբ ճեռից,
Սեւ ամպ էր իջել Սասունի վրայ։

— Հոդե՛մ, գլյուխարդ, — ասաւ կնիկբ, —
Ո՛վ գիտի՝ Դաւիթն ո՛ւր է քէջ անում...
Դու էլ քեզ Համար քու տանբ քնած՝
Ուրիշի Համար երազ ես տեսնում։

Քնեց Օհանբ։ Վերկացաւ դարձեալ․
— Կնի՛կ, Դաւիթբ նեղ տեղն է ընկած․
Մարայ վառ աստղբ հողում էր պայծառ,
Մեր աստղբ Հիանդ ցոլում դալկացած։

— Ի՞նչ եղաւ քեզ, մա՛րդ, գիշերուան կիսին, —
Բարկացաւ վրբին կնիկն ադմուկով։
Խաչ քաշեց էլ ետ Օհանն երեսին,
Շուռ եկաւ, քնեց խռոված հոգով։

Մի ուրիշ պատկեր աւելի աճեղ
Տեսաւ՝ երկնքի բարձր կամարում
Վաուում էր Մարայ աստղբ փարաՀեղ,
Սասմայ աստղիկբ սուզուեց խաւարում։

Զարթնեց վախեցած։ — Տունդ քանդուի, կի՛ն,
Ես ո՞նց լբսեցի քու էդ կարճ խելբին․

He would coax them to sit in his great tent,
Directly over those black and deadly wells.

Dismounting from his horse, David came near,
He went in, he sat, he fell into a well.
Ha, ha, ha, ha, ho ho, ho ho, hee hee,
Laughed the king of Egypt, Egypt's merciless king.

"There, now let him sit, let him stay in that dark
Well till he rots away, and more."
Saying this, he brought an immense millstone,
An enormous millstone, and rolled it over the well.

XXII

On that same night big-voiced Ohan slept.
He dreamt that there appeared, in the sky
Over Egypt, a bright sun streaming bright rays,
But a black cloud loomed over Sassoun's fastness.

Ohan was terror-stricken. Up from his bed
He sprang. "O wife, bring up a light," he said.
"Our artless David has bolted again,
And a black cloud hangs over Sassountown."

"May the earth fall on your head!" said his wife.
"Who knows how or where David is, having fun,
Yet here you are asleep in your cozy home,
Seeing dreams and worrying about others."

Ohan fell asleep, but again he started:
"O wife, David has come to narrow straits.
Egypt's bright star glimmers brilliantly,
But our star glows yellowish and sickly."

"What's come over you, man, in the middle of
The night?" his wife shouted furiously.
Ohan crossed himself again upon the face,
Turned over, and slept, though with a troubled heart.

He had another dream, more fearful than
Before: from heaven's high arch now sparkled,
Resplendently, Egypt's star; Sassoun's
Little star waned and sank slowly toward the dark.

He woke up, afraid. "Wife, may your house be wrecked!
How could I listen to your witless chatter!

Կորաւ մեն մենակ մեր ջահիլն անտէր․
Վե՛ր կաց, չո՛լտ արա, գէնքերս մի բե՛ր...

XXIII

Ելաւ Օհան, գոմը մտաւ,
Զարկեց ճերմակ ձիու մէջքե՛ն․
—է՛յ, ճերմակ ձի, մինչ ե՞րբ, — ասաւ, —
Կը հասցնես Դալթի կռուին։

«Մինչեւ լուս կը հասցնեմ»․
Ու ձին տուաւ փորը գետին․
—Մէջքդ կոտրի՛, լուսն ի՞նչ անեմ․
Լային հասնեմ ես թէ՞ նաշին։

Կարմիր ձիու մէջքին զարկեց․
Սա էլ երեւ փորը գետին։
—Ջա՛ն կարմիր ձի, մինչ ե՞րբ դու ինձ
Կը հասցնես Դալթի կռուին։

«Մի՛ ժամի մէջ, — կարմիրն ասաւ, —
Կը հասցնեմ Դալթի կռուին»։
—Լեղի դառնայ, սեւ մաշ ուցաւ,
Ինչ տուել եմ քեզ՝ էն գարին։

Հերթը եկաւ՝ սեւին հասաւ․
Գետին չերեւ փորը սեւ ձին։
—է՛յ, ջան Սեւուկ, մինչ ե՞րբ, — ասաւ, —
Կը հասցնես Դալթի կռուին։

«Եթէ ամուր մէջքիս մնաս,
Ուղղ դնես ասպանդակին,
Մինչեւ մէկել ուղղ շուռ տաս,
Կը հասցնեմ», ասաւ սեւ ձին։

XXIV

Սեւ ձին քաչեց Չէնով Օհան,
Ջախը դրաւ ասպանդակին,
Աչն էլ մինչեւ շուռ տար վրան,
Կանգնեց Սասմայ սարի գլխին։

Տեսաւ՝ Դալթի նժոյգն անտէր
Սարերն ընկած խրինջալով,
Ներքեւ Մսրայ գորքը շոքած։
Ինչպէս անձայր ծփուն մի ծով։

Alone, by himself our orphaned young
David is lost now. Up! Get up, bring me my arms."

XXIII

Ohan rose and went to the barn
And gave his white horse a pat on the back.
"Well, white horse," he said, "how long will it be
Before you can take me where David fights?"

"You shall be there by dawn," and saying this,
The white horse brought its belly to the ground.
"May your back be broken! What'll I do at dawn,
View his corpse or attend his funeral?"

He gave the red horse a pat on the back.
That horse, too, brought its belly to the ground.
"O red horse," he said, "how long will it be
Before you can take me where David fights?"

"You shall be there in one hour," the red horse said,
"In one hour I can take you where David fights."
"May your gall burst! Pain and death take you!
Alas for all that barley you have eaten."

And now it was the turn of the black horse;
The black horse brought its belly to the ground, too.
"O my little black one, how long will it be,"
He said, "before you can take me where David fights?"

"If you can stay fast on my back," the black
Horse said, "by the time you have one foot in the
Stirrup and before you have the other one thrown over,
I will have brought you where David fights."

XXIV

The black horse swiftly dragged big-voiced Ohan;
He placed his left foot in the stirrup,
And by the time he threw his right foot over,
The black horse had brought him to the highlands.

Now Ohan saw David's unmounted steed,
Roaming in the highlands and neighing aloud;
He saw the Egyptian encampment below,
Undulating endlessly, like the sea.

Օխտը գոմշի կաշի հագաւ,
Որ չպատռի իրեն դօթից,
Կանդնեց Օհան, ամպի նման
Գոռաց Սասմայ սարի ձերից։

—Հէ՛յ-հէ՛յ Դալի՛թ, ո՛րտեղ ես դու.
Ցիշի՛ր խաչը պատարագի,
Սուրբ Տիրամօր անունը տո՛ւր,
Լո՛ւսը դուր է՛կ արեգակի։

Չէնը դնաց, դղմըդմըալով՝
Դալիթի ականջն ընկաւ հօրում.
—Հա՛-հա՛յ, — ասաւ, — հօրեղբայրս է,
Սասմայ սարից ինձ է գոռում։

Օ՛վ Մարութայ Աստուածին,
Օ՛վ անմահ խաչ պատարագի,
Զե՛ զ եմ կանչել, — հասէ՛ք Դալիթին —,
Կանչեց, տեղից կանդնեց ոտքի,

էնպէս գարկեց ջաղացքարին՝
Քարը եղաւ հազար կտոր,
Կտորները երկինք թռան,
Ու դնում են մինչեւ էսօր։

Ելաւ հորից, կանդնեց աձեղ։
Սարափ կալաւ դեւ Մելիքին։
—Դալիթ ախպէր, ե՛կ դեռ էստեղ,
Սեղան նստե՛նք, խօսենք կարգի՛ն...

—էլ չեմ նստիլ ես քու հացին,
Դու տմարդի, վախկոտ ու նենգ.
Շո՛ւտ, դէնքըրդ առ, հեձիր քու ձին,
Դո՛ւրս եկ մէյդան, կռիւ անենք։

—Կռիւ անենք, — ասաւ Մելիք, —
Իմն է միայն գարկն առաջին.
—Քոնն է, գարկի՛ր, — կանչեց Դալիթ,
Գնաց, կեցաւ դաշտի միջին։

Ելաւ, կանդնեց Սրա-Մելիք,
Իր գուրզն առաւ, հեձաւ իր ձին,
Քշեց, դնաց մինչ Դիարպեքիր
Ու էնտեղից եկաւ կրկին։

That all these might not burst with his straining,
Ohan put on the skins of seven oxen.
And Ohan stood, like a cloud, on the top of the
Highest peak in Sassoun's highlands, and roared:

"O David, O David, where can you be!
Only remember the cross on your arm, speak
The name of our Blessed Madonna
And come out into the daylight."

His voice carried, reverberated,
And echoed strongly in David's inner ear.
"Ho ho! That is my uncle's voice," he said,
"He is calling me from Sassoun's fastnesses.

O blessed Madonna of Marouta,
O intrepid cross of our litany,
I call on you now—succor David now,"
He cried, and rose to his feet in the well.

With such strength, with such force did he strike the millstone,
That the stone was smashed into a thousand pieces;
The pieces flew up to high heaven,
And they are still in flight to this day.

The formidable Melik came out of his lair,
His fiendish spirit was possessed by fear.
"Brother David, do come over here, still,
Let's sit at table together and parley."

"Never again will I sit with you at table,
You base, you crooked, you craven man;
Quick, get up, take up your arms, mount your horse,
Come out into the open and let us fight."

"Indeed, let's fight, let's fight," Melik said,
"But it is my right to strike the first blow."
"Oh, very well, it's yours, strike," David called;
He walked out and stood in the middle of the plain.

Musra-Melik rose, he got to his feet,
Took up his lance, mounted his horse,
And dashed off all the way to Diarbekir,
And then from that place returned.

Երեք հազար լիդր էր քաշում
Հակայական իր մկունդը.*
Եկավ, զարկեց. կորավ փոշում
Ու երերաց երկրի գունդը:

Երկիր քանդուեց կամ ժամք եղավ՝
Ասին մարդիկ շատ աշխարքում:
—Չէ՛,— ասացին, արնի ծարավ
Հականերն են իրար զարկում:
—Մեռավ Դավիթ էս մի զարկից,—
Ասաւ Մելիք իրեն գործքին:
—Կենդանի ե՛մ, ամպի տակից—
Գոռաց Դավիթ Մսրա-Մելքին:

—Հա՛յ–հա՛յ, մոտիկ տեղից եկայ,
Տե՛ս, ո՛րտեղից հիմի կը գամ՝
Ու վերկացավ, կանգնեց Հական,
Իր ձին հեծավ երկրորդ անգամ:

Երկրորդ անգամ քշեց Հալաբ
Ու բաց թողեց ձին Հալաբից.
Բուք վերկացավ, տեղ ու տարափ,
Արաբ աշխարհ դողաց թափից:

Եկավ, զարկեց. զարկի ձենից
Մոտիկ մարդիկ ոչ խլացան:
—Գնա՛ց Դավիթ Սասմայ տանից,—
Գուժեց գուռող Մսրայ արքան:

—Կենդանի՛ եմ,— կանչեց Դավիթ,—
Մին էլ արի՛— Հերթն ինձ հասաւ:
—Հա՛–հա՛յ, մոտիկ տեղից եկայ,
Կանչեց Մելիք ու վերկացավ:

Երրորդ անգամ հեծավ իր ձին,
Գնաց մինչեւ հողը Մսրայ,
Ու ջնտեղից, գուրզը ձեռին
Քշեց, եկաւ Դավթի վրայ:

Եկավ, զարկեց բոլոր ուժով,
Ծանրը զարկով հակայական.
Փոշին ելաւ Սասմայ դաշտից,
Բռնեց երեսն արեգական:

Երեք գիշեր ու երեք օր
Փոշին կանգնեց ամպի նման,
$Գուրդ.

Թումանեան / 206

Melik was drawing three thousand boulders
By the handle of his gigantic lance.
He charged and struck a blow—at once the dust
Rose and the world trembled mightily.

"There's been an earthquake or the world's destroyed,"
People shouted throughout the world;
"No," others said, "bloodthirsty giants,
Mighty men are locked in battle."
"From this single blow only, David has died,"
Musra-Melik told his countless soldiers,
But David called from beneath a cloud,
"Musra-Melik, I am still among the quick!"

"Well, I charged from a short distance only
But now you'll see from where I come!"
The mighty one rose, came to his feet,
And sprang on his mount for the second time.

He rode clear to Aleppo the second time,
And on his way back left the reins free,
Rains came, and hail, and a strong hurricane
Shook the earth with tremendous force.

He came, he struck, and from the clamor of
The blow, bystanders were completely deafened.
"David is lost to the House of David,"
The haughty Egyptian king announced.

"I am still among the quick," shouted David,
"Charge once again—but no, it's my turn now."
"Well, I charged from short distance only,"
Melik shouted, and sprang on his mount.

For the third time now he mounted his horse;
He rode away to Egypt's own soil,
And from that distance, lance in hand,
He rode back, charging full tilt at David.

He charged at David and struck with all his strength,
Struck with a crushing and formidable blow,
The dust went as high as Sassoun's peaks,
Its denseness hid the face of the sun.

For three nights and three days, the dust hung
Over the countryside like a cloud.

Երեք գիշեր ու երեք օր
Թօթը տուին Դաւթի մահուան։

Երբ որ անցաւ երեք օրը,
էն ամպի պես կանգնած փոշում
Կանգնեց Դաւիթ, ինչպես սարը,
Գրգուռ սարը մէգ-մշուշում։

— Մելի՛ք, — ասաւ, — ո՞ւմն է հերթը։ —
Սարսափ կալաւ գող Մելիքին,
Մահուան դողը ընկաւ սիրտը
Ու տապ արաւ գործող հոգին։

Գնաց, խորունկ մի հոր փորեց,
Իջաւ, մտաւ վիշն էն խաւար,
Վրէն քաշեց քառասուն կաշի
Ու քառասուն ջաղացի քար։

Մռնչալով ելաւ տեղից
էն առիւծի առիւծ որդին,
Իր ճին հեծաւ ու փոթորկեց,
Խաղաց, ցողաց Թուր-Կայծակին։

Առաջ վազեց մագերն արձակ
Մելքի պառաւ մայրը ջաղու.
— Դաւի՛թ, մագրս ա՛ռ ութիդ տակ,
էդ մի գարկը ի՛նձ բաշխիր դու։

Երկրորդ անգամ թուրը քաշեց.
էս անգամ էլ եկաւ քուրը.
— Դաւի՛թ, եթէ կ՚ուզես, — կանչեց,
Իմ սրտին գա՛րկ երկրորդ թուրը...

Վերջին գարկի ժամը հասաւ,
Ելաւ Դաւիթ երրորդ անգամ.
— էս մի գարկն ու Աստուած, — ասաւ, —
էլ մարդ չգա՛յ, պէտք է որ տամ։

Ասաւ, ելաւ ու փոթորկեց,
Թռաւ, ցոլաց Դաւթի հուր ճին,
Ճին փոթորկեց, փայլատակեց
Ու գաց իջաւ Թուր-Կայծակին։

Անցաւ քառասուն գոմշի կաշին,
Անցաւ քառասուն քարերը գած,

For three nights and three days, rumors
Went forth that David of Sassoun had died.

When three days had passed, like the dust
That remained cloudlike, David too remained;
Yes, as the high peak, the peak of Mount Kur-Kur,
So stood David, fog shrouded and majestic.

"O Melik," he roared, "whose turn is it now?"
Melik's proud soul was terror-stricken:
Death's tremors now shook him to his very heart,
His haughty, puffed up spirit was now sunken.

Melik strode forth and dug himself a deep well,
He eased himself down into the dark hole,
Covered its opening with forty skins,
And covered even these with forty millstones.

That lion-hearted son of the lion-hearted,
David, rose from where he'd sat grumbling,
Mounted his restless horse and made it career,
As he held high his gleaming lightning sword.

Now came forth, her hair loosed before her,
Melik's mother, a cruel, a nasty old woman,
"O David, by my hair draw me under
Your heels, but let your first blow fall on me."

A second time he lifted his sword high;
Musra-Melik's sister came running.
"O David, if you wish," she called,
"Strike your second blow on my trembling heart."

Now the hour had come for the final blow,
And for the third time David raised his sword.
"This one blow alone I strike for God's sake.
I must strike," he said, "no one else remains."

Saying this, he mounted and careered his horse.
His fiery steed rose up and flew high,
Careered defiantly in the heavens—
And then the sword of lightning came down.

It passed through forty hides of oxen,
And it passed through forty millstones,

Մի֊չից կտրեց ժանտ հրեշին,
Օխտը գագ էլ դէնը դնաց։
—Կենդանի՛ եմ, մին էլ արի՛, —
Գոռաց Մելիք Հորի տակից։
Դալիթ լսեց, շատ զարմացաւ
Իրեն գարկից, Թուր-Կայծակից...

—Մելի՛ք, — ասաւ, — թա՛փ տուր մի քեզ։ —
Ու թափ տուաւ Մելիքն իրեն,
Մի֊չից եղաւ ճիչդ երկու կէս,
Մէկն ընկաւ դեան ու միւսը դէն։

Էս որ տեսաւ Մսրայ բանակ,
Զուր կոբրուեց աչ ու վախից։
Դալիթ կանչեց. — Մի՛ վախենաք,
Ակա՛նչ արէք հալա դեռ ինձ։

Դուք լռանչպար մարդիկ, — ասաւ, —
Զուրկ ու խաւար, քաղցած ու մերկ,
Հազար ու մի կրակ ու ցաւ,
Հազար ու մի հոգսեր ունէք։

Ի՞նչ էք առել նետ ու աղեղ,
Եկել թափել օտար դաշտեր․
Չէ՞ որ մենք էլ ունենք տուն-տեղ,
Մենք էլ ունենք մանուկ ու ծեր...

Զանգրացե՞լ էք խաղաղ ու հաշտ
Հողագործի օր ու կեանքից,
Թէ՞ գզուել էք ձեր հանդ ու դաշտ,
Ձեր հունձ ու փունչ, վար ու ցանքից...

Դարձէ՛ք եկած ճանապարհով
Ձեր հայրենի հողը Մսրայ․
Բայց թէ մին էլ գէնք ու զօրով
Վեր էք կացել դուք մեզ վրա՛յ,

Հորո՛ւմ լինեն քարսուն գագ խոր,
Թէ չաղացի քարի տակին, —
Կ՛ելնեն ձեր դէմ, ինչպէս այսօր,
Սասմայ Դալի՛թ, Թո՛ւր-Կայծակին։

Էն ժամանակ, Աստուա՛ծ գիտի,
Ո՛վ մեզանից կ՛ըլնի փոշման.
Մե՞նք, որ կ՛ելնենք աշեղ մարտի,
Թէ դուք, որ մեզ արիք դուշման...

It struck clear through the loathsome monster,
And scattered its halves for seven spans.

"I am still among the quick! Strike once again,"
Melik roared from deep in the well.
David heard and was much astonished,
After the blow he'd struck with his lightning sword.

"Do move about a bit, Melik," he said,
And Melik stirred inside the well.
Right down the middle he was cut in two,
One half falling here, the other there.

When the Egyptian soldiers beheld this sight,
Their blood to water turned, they were terror-struck.
David called, "Do not be afraid, any of you,
But listen to what I say.

You are only farmers, tillers of the soil,
Denied and benighted, hungry, naked,
With a thousand and one ills and pains,
With a thousand and one troubles to boot;

Why have you taken up bows and arrows,
And spilled onto far and alien plains?
Don't you know that we, too, have homes and hearths,
We, too, have tender infants and aged folk?

Are you tired of the quiet and peaceful life,
The peaceful, quiet life of the farmer?
Are you tired of the threshing floor, the field,
Tillage and sowing, and your harvests and green crops?

Return by the paths that brought you here,
Return to your native soil, Egypt;
But if by might and in arms
You dare again to march against these freeborn men,

Be the wells you dig forty measures deep,
Be they covered over with forty millstones,
Against you will rise, just as today,
David of Sassoun and his lightning sword.

And only God will know, at that time,
Who between us shall the sorrier be:
We who rise up to wage great battle,
Or you who've made of us your enemy."

Աւետիք Իսահակեան

Avetik Issahakian

1875–1957

Թավեննայում

Արարատի ձեր կատարին
Դարե է եկել, վայրկեանի պես,
Ու անցել։

Անհուն թւով կայծակների
Սուրն է բեկուել ադամանդին,
Ու անցել։

Մահասուճապ սերունդների
Աչքն է դիպել լույս գագաթին,
Ու անցել։

Հերթը հիմա քո՛նն է մի պահ.
Դո՛ւ էլ նայիր սեգ ճակատին,
Ու անցի՛ր...

Որտե՞ղ է Ընկած

Որտե՞ղ է ընկած
Այն քարը հիմի,
Որ հոգիս վրայ
Շիրիմ պիտ լինի։

Իմ թափառ կեանքում,
Մարդ ի՞նչ իմանայ,
Չե՞մ նստել, թախծել
Այդ քարի վրայ...

From Ravenna

Across the hoary crest of Ararat,
Centuries have rolled, like a minute,
And passed on.

The lightning swords of countless storms
Have been shattered on its rock
And passed on.

The eyes of generations, in death-throes,
Have looked on its gleaming peak
And passed on.

Now, for a time, it is your turn—
You, too, must look at its proud brow
And pass on.

Where Does the Stone Lie?

Where does the stone
Lie, now,
That will be
The headstone over my grave?

Who can tell,
In my roaming life,
I've not sat, grieving,
On that stone?

Գետակի Վրայ

Գետակի վրայ
Թեքուել է ուռին
Ու նայում է լուռ
Վազող ջրերին։

...Երազ-աշխարհում
Ամէն բան յաւէտ
Գալիս է, գնում
Ու ցնդում անհետ։

Եւ գլուխը կախ՝
Նա լաց է լինում. —
Ջրերը ուրախ՝
Գալիս են, գնում...

Over the Stream

Over the stream
The willow is bent,
It stares in silence
On the running water.

In this dream world
All things are forever
Coming and going away,
Fading away, traceless.

And with its head bowed
The willow weeps—
The laughing water keeps
Coming and going away.

Վահան Թէքէեան

Vahan Tekeyan

1878–1945

Հանրմը

Միակտուր սեւ-անփայլ մետաքսն ամբողջ զինք ծածկած
Եւ քայլերուն մետաքսէ խոր շրշիւնվը թեթեւ,
Որ ազդերուն քնարին կարծես նուագն բլար ցած,
Կ'երթայ հանըրմն՝ յուզելով մուշկի ալիք մ'իր եառեւ:

Ժանեկագարդ թելեն դուրս կը բխի ճեռքը ազաթիկ,
Չոր նախանձոտ սեւ ճեռնոց մը կը պատհէ կիսովին,
Մինչ ուղղանկիւն ճակատին ինկած քօղն ալ լուսանցիկ
Մանրածարիր աչքերուն կ'անթեղէ հուրքը խորին:

Կամուրջին վրայ յորդագեղ վերճալոյսի մը ներքեւ,
Կ'երթայ հանըրմը այսպէս, հորիզոնէ հորիզոն,
Մթնչելով Ոսկեղջիւրն ու դիւթելով երեկոն...

Կ'երթայ հանըրմն՝ անմատո՛յց, քօղածածո՛ւկ, հոյածէ՛լ,
Կին կամ ոգի, պաճ մ'եղած պալատներէն Պոլիսի,
Պոյսոյ ոգի՛ն, խուսափուկ, անքննելի՛, սխրալի՛...։

Աղուորները

Աղուորն ա՛ն չ յալիտեան, որ անցաւ օր մը քովէդ
Եւ աչունե՛րըդ օձեց, — աստուածային այցելո՛ւ, —
Գեղեցկութեամբ մը, որուն ա՛լ չդարձար նայելու,
Եւ չուղեցիր հանդիպել անոր անգամ մըն ալ գէթ...

Աղուորն ա՛ն չ տակալին, — յալիտեանէ յալիտեան, —
Որ նայուածքիդ արեւին տակ կը մեծնար յամրօրէն,
Որ դերթ ծաղիկ մ'օրօրող գարնան անուշ հովերէն,
Երբ մեկնեցաւ մոքիդ մէչ մնաց մի՛շտ թարմ, մի՛շտ բուրեան..

Եւ աղուո'րբը, — դուն գիտե'ս օրհնեալ անունբը անոր, —
Անիկա' է, որ կարծես պիտի կրնար քեզ սիրել,
Որ սէրդ անչուշտ դուչակեց եւ սպասե'ց ակնկոր,

Որուն սակայն լալ է, որ չուղեցիր սիրտը խուովել...
Աղուորն անո՛նք են միայն, որ տենչանքթիդ ընդմէջէն
Անցան, դացի՛ն ու հիմա քեզ հեռուէն կը կանչեն...։

The Hanoum

Entirely draped in a black silk unlustrous gown,
Her footsteps light under deep rushes of silk,
A rustling like a lute song down her thighs,
The hanoum goes forth, trailing a cloud of musk.

A small hand flashes from her jewelled arm,
A hand half-covered by a black jealous glove,
While the delicate veil, drawn over her symmetrical forehead,
Lends her deep eyes the fireglow of a censer.

Across a bridge, beneath the rich sunset,
The hanoum goes forth, from horizon to horizon,
Outshining the Golden Horn and enchanting the Eventide . . .

The hanoum goes unhampered, veiled, magnificent,
Woman or spirit, abroad for a moment from Istanbul's castles,
The spirit of Istanbul—secret, audacious, unknowable.

Hanoum refers to a woman of refinement, a lady.

The Beautiful Ones

The beautiful one is always she who walked past you one day
And anointed your eyes—a divine visitor,
You failed to turn and look back at such beauty,
And you did not wish to meet her again.

The beautiful one is forever, always and ever,
She who grew into grace under the warmth of your eyes,
Who swayed like a flower in the sweet spring winds,
And when you went away, she stayed always fresh in your mind, ever
                                                                                            fragrant.

And the beautiful one—you know her delightful name—
Is she who might have loved you after all,
Who certainly guessed your love and waited eagerly for you,

But she is one whose heart it's just as well you did not wound—
Ah, the beautiful ones are only they who through your desires
Came and went away, but who call you now from afar . . .

Սիամանթօ
Siamanto (Adom Yarjanian)
1878–1915

Ափ մը Մոխիր, Հայրենի Տուն...

Ա

Առա՛ջ, ապարանքի մը պէս մեծ էիր եւ շքեղ,
Ու ես՝ երդիքներուդ սպիտակ կատարէն,
Աստղածորան գիշերներու լոյսին հետ,
Վարէն, աճեղավագ Եփրատին կ'ունկնդրէի...։

Բ

Արցունքո՛վ, արցունքո՛վ լցեցի որ աւերակ առ աւերակ
Քու լայնանիստ պատերդ իրարու վրայ կործանեցին,
Սարսափի օր մը, կոտորածի օր մը, օր մը ապրիւնի...
Զքեզ եզերող պարտէզիդ ծաղկըներուն վրայ։

Գ

Ու մոխրացա՞ւ այն սենեակը կապոյտ,
Որուն որմերուն եռեւ եւ գորգերուն վրայ
Իմ երջանիկ մանկութիւնս կը հրճուէր,
Եւ կեանքս կ'աճէր եւ հոգիս իր թեւերը կ'առնէր...

Դ

Փշրեցա՞ւ, ուրեմն, այն հայելին ոսկեծիր,
Որուն եթերային խորութեանը մէջ,
Երազներս, յոյսերս, սէրերս եւ կամքս կարմիր,
Տարիներով, մտածումիս հետ, ցոլացին...։

Ե

Ու բակին մէջ երգող աղբիւրը մեռա՞ւ,
Ու կոտրտեցա՞ն պարտէզիս ուռին եւ թթենին.
Եւ այն առուակը որ ծառերուն մէջէն կը հոսէր,
Ցամքեցա՞ւ, բայց, ո՞րր է, ցամքեցա՞ւ, ցամքեցա՞ւ...

Զ

Օ՛, այն վանդակին կ'երազեմ յաճախ,
Որուն մէջ գործազոյն կաքաւս, առաւօտուն,
Արեւածագին հետ եւ վարդի թուփերուն դիմաց,
Զարթնումի ժամուս՝ յստակօրէն կը կարգնէր...

Սիամանթօ / 224

A Handful of Ash

(a)

Alas, you were a great and beautiful mansion,
And from the white summit of your roof,
Filled with star-flooded night hopes,
I listened to the Euphrates, racing below.

(b)

I learned with tears, with tears I learned of the ruins,
Of your broad walls battered down, stone by stone,
Onto your fragile border of flowers in the garden . . .
On a terror-filled day, a day of slaughter, of blood.

(c)

And charred is the blue room
Inside whose walls, on whose rugs
My childhood delighted,
And where my life grew, where my soul grew.

(d)

That gold-framed mirror is shattered, too,
In whose silver depth my dreams,
My hopes, my loves and my burning will
Stood reflected for years, and my musings.

(e)

And in the garden the spring song is dead,
The mulberry and the willow there, they have been blasted, too,
And the brook that flowed between the trees—
Has it gone dry? Tell me, where is it? Has it gone dry?

(f)

O I often dream of the cage
From which my grey partridge, mornings
And at sunrise, fronting the rose trees,
Would rise, as I did, and start its own distinct cooing.

Է

Հայրենի՛ տուն, հաւատա՛ որ մահէս յետոյ,
Քու աւերակներուդ սեւին վայ իմ հոգիս
Պիտի գայ, որպէս տատրակ մը տարագիր,
Իր դժբախտի երգն եւ արցունքը լալու...։

Ը

Բայց ո՛վ պիտի բերէ, ո՛վ պիտի բերէ, ըսէ՛,
Քու սրբազան մոխիրէդ ափ մը մոխիր,
Մահուանս օրը, իմ տրտում դագաղիս մէջ,
Հայրենիքս երգողի իմ աճիւնին խառնելու...

Թ

Ափ մը մոխի՛ր աճիւնիս հետ, Հայրենի տուն,
Ափ մը մոխի՛ր քու մոխիրէդ, ո՛վ պիտի բերէ,
Քու յիշատակէ՛դ, քու ցաւէ՛դ, քու անցեալէ՛դ,
Ափ մը մոխիր... իմ սրտիս վրան ցանելու...։

(g)

O my homeland, promise that after my death
A handful of your holy ashes
Will come to rest, like an exiled turtledove,
To chant its song of sorrow and tears.

(h)

But who will bring, tell me, who is to bring
A handful of your precious ashes,
On the day of my death, to put into my dark coffin
And mingle with my ashes, ashes of a singer of the homeland?

(i)

A handful of ash with my remains, my native home—
Who is to bring a handful of ash from your ashes,
From your sorrow, your memories, your past,
A handful of ash to scatter on my heart?

Դանիէլ Վարուժան
Daniel Varoujan
1884–1915

Աշակները

Աշակներն են իմ գիւղիս, դաշտի հզո՛ր պալակներ,
Քրտինքներով մարգարտեայ՝ բնութեան թա՛գն են Հիւսեր։
Կը բաբախէ սիրտն հողին իրենց բրդոտ կուրծքին տակ.
Ու իրենց լայն երակին մէջ կը յորդի արեգակ։

Երբ որ քալեն՝ մայր-երկիրն իր արգանդէն կը սարսայ.
Բայց չի խամրիր ծիլ մը իսկ գարշապարնուն տակ Հակայ։
Գլուխն իրենց, զոր կ'Հակեն առջեւը սուրբ խորանին,
Պսակուած է միշտ ոսկի փոշիներովը յարդին։

Ակօսներուն մէջ, անոնք խի՛նդ կը ցանեն, եւ Աստուած
Իրենց ճակտին ակօսէն բարութիւններ կը Հնձէ։
Աւիշներու Հոսուն երգն անոնք միայն են լսած։

Եգին շողիքն, ի՛նչ փոյթ թէ իրենց ձեռքերը կ'ոծէ,
Եւ ախորի Հոտ կու գայ իրենց նախշուն լօդիկէն. —
Նախ անոնց լա՛յն ափին մէջ կը ծլին սերմերն Համօրէն։

Առկայծ ճրագ

Ցաղթանակի գիշերն է այս տօնական. —
Հա՛րս, եղ լեցուր ճրագին։
Պիտի դառնայ կռիւէն տղաս յաղթական. —
Հա՛րս, քիթը ա՛ռ պատրոյգին։

Սայլ մը կեցաւ դրան առջեւ, Հորին քով. —
Հա՛րս, վառէ' լոյսը ճրագին։
Տղաս կու գայ ճակտան Հպարտ դափնիով. —
Հա՛րս, բե՛ր ճըրագը շեմին։

Բայց... սայլին վրայ արիւն եւ սո°ւգ բեռցեր են...
Հա՛րս, ճրագդ ասդի՛ն երկարէ։
Հերոս տղաս Հոն գարնուա՛ծ է սրտէն. —
Ա՛խ, Հա՛րս, ճրագդ մարէ'...

Tillers

They are the mighty children of the fields,
The tillers of the soil who live around my town,
Who weave with pearly sweat Nature's precious crown;
Beneath their swaying strength the soil pulses,
And in their broadened veins the sunrays course.
And when they walk heavily across
The fields not a single shoot is bruised,
But the earth itself trembles from its core.
Their heads are never bowed before the shrine,
But are flecked with the golden dust of straw.
They sow mirth among the furrows,
And God finds only goodness in the furrows
Of their brow; the song of the rising sap
And growing bud is the only song they know.
What if the oxen's froth is on their hands,
And their tattered cloaks reek of the stable—
The living seeds first sprout in their palms.

The Flickering Lamp

This is a night for feast and triumph,
   Pour oil into the lamp, O Bride,
My boy returns a victor from war—
   Trim well, trim well the wick, O Bride.

A wagon stops before the door, beside the well,
   Light up, light up the lamp, O Bride,
My boy returns, bay leaves on his brow—
   Bring up, bring up the lamp, O Bride.

Lo—with grief and blood the wagon's laden—
   Hold up, hold up the lamp, O Bride.
Here lies my valiant son shot through the heart—
   Oh . . . snuff out, snuff out the lamp, O Bride.

Արեւելեան Բաղանիք

Մորձագմբէթ բաղնիքին ներքնադուռն յո՛յլ կը բացուի,
Եբենոս դռ՛լուն հաստաբեստ՝ որ կը ծեծուի միշտ թակով,
Եւ անընդհատ կը քրտնի, կը ճռնչէ ուժասպառ
Հուրիներուն եւեւէն՝ որոնք դանդա՛ղ կը մտնեն.
Բոլոր մե՛րկ են ու չքնա՛ղ, — թեւերն իրենց ծալլեր են
Լանջքերնուն վրայ հոյաշէն՝ որոնց վրայ կը դիզուին
Կոյտերն իրենց ծիծերուն, պտուկներով թխագեղ։
Սատափագոծ սանդալներն յատակին վրայ կը հնչեն.
Արտերնուն հեւքն ադուական, ճայներն իրենց քաղցրանոյշ
Բաղնիքէն ներս կը փոխուին անդնդասույզ ղօղանջի.
Աստղերուն պէս՝ լողացող մառախուղին մէջ աղօտ՝
Իրենց աչքերը խոնաւ նշոյլներներ կ՚արձակեն,
Եւ գլուխշին, իր տամուկ շղարշներով, կը պատէ
Մարմինն իրենց՝ որ պողիլ կը սկսի ա՛լ քրտինքով։
Հուրիները կը լոգնա՛ն. — Պորտաքարին կիզանուտ
Ոմանք պառկած նուաղկոտ նայուածքներով կ՚երազեն.
Լուսացնցուղ գմբէթէն՝ արեւուն շողը ճերմակ
Ներս կը մաղուի՝ մարգարտեայ յորդ անձրեւի մը նման.
Եւ ծխանուտ գոլորշին կը դառնայ ծով մ՚արծաթեայ
Ուր լիւղ կոու գան կարապներն Արեւելքի Հեշտանքին.
Ըսպածանին՝ որ կապած է գոտերնուն լօդ պէս,
Ա՛լ կը նետուի. մարմինները կը փոխուին արձանի.
Եւ մագերնին, հիւս առ հիւս, ծովերու պէս կը քակեն,
Ուրկէ երբե՛մ՚ըն կ՚իյնան գոհարներու հատիկներ։
Օ՛, ծամե՛րն այդ, ծամե՛րն այդ, որոնցմով ա՛լ կը ծփայ
Կարծես բաղնիքը ամբողջ. եւ պորտաքարը մարմար
Կը թխանայ անոնց յորդ սեւափրփուր ալիքով։

Oriental Bath

The inner door of the green-domed bath opens slowly,
And as it grates and sweats all day,
Against its massive ebony frame pound
Heavy pendant pulley weights,
That now swing into a wide, true arc,
Inviting in a cluster of naked houris,
Who drift in, lingeringly, slowly;
All naked, and all surpassing beautiful,
Their arms folded modestly
Across their gleaming breasts, which swell
Over and onto their forearms, breasts darkly starred
With round brown nipples, swaying breasts;
Their wooden sandals, worked in mother of pearl,
Clink sharply on the damp, cool marble floor;
Inside the bath their low melodious voices
And their soft breath turn to muffled bells.
And as the vapor rises within
The bath, like moistened veils clinging
Along their naked bodies, which now start to pearl
With sweat, their eyes glow with a fine warm luster,
Like brilliant stars seen through a foggy sky.
Houris at their baths! Some, stretched out
On warm navelstones, dream, smiling languorously,
While from the light-spreading dome the sun
Filters through like pearly rain,
Making a lustrous sea of the dense
Silver vapors in which swim these sinuous
Swans, Oriental maidens; and now they cast
Aside the towels that had clung like seaweed
To their thighs—Oh, their bodies unadorned as statues!
And now their hair, braid on braid, like waves
On a stormy sea, loosened,
And at intervals precious stones escape,
That hair, Oh, that hair,
The whole bath seems to undulate, darkening
With its raven sway the white and granite

Navelstones are body length slabs of marble, found in the bathhouses of Asia Minor. The bathers recline on them during ablutions.

Գլուխն իրենց կը սանտրեն ոսկեղրուագ սանտրերով
Երկա՛ր, երկա՛ր, մինչեւ ծայրն անծայրածիր մազերուն
Կ՚երթան իրենց մատուղները ձեռձեքուն ու դանդաղ
Միշտ լողալով կայծերու մէջ մատնիի անդամանդ։
Անոնք երբե՛մն կը զգան նուաղումներ, ու երբեմն
Ցանկարձակի կը սարսռան՝ երբ գմբէթէն կը կաթի
Ցուրտ ցօղ մ՚իրենց ձօծրակին Հեշտագրգիո փոսին մէջ։
ԱՀա Հարիւր ձօրակնե՛րն, աՀա մարմար ձօրակնե՛րն
Իրար ետեւ կը բացուին՝ աղմկայոյզ կարկաչով.
Մոխիրի պէս գորշ շոգին կը բարձրանայ ձուփ առ ձուփ.
Դատարկ գուռերը բոլոր կենդանութիւն կը ստանան.
Ջուրը կ՚յորդի ամէն կողմ, ջուրը կ՚երգէ քաղցրաՀունչ.
Հուրիները կը լողնա՛ն. — Գուռերուն շուրջ Հաւաքուած
Գանովայի՛ Շնորհներ, կարծես իրար կը փարին,
Եւ կը խառնեն ծիծերնին, կը խառնեն ժիր թեւերնին
Եւ սրունքնին պաղպաջուն, եւ պորտերնին կօշարայ՝
Ուրկէ մուշկի Հատիկներ, տարրալուծուած, կը բուրեն։
Մարմարներուն վրայ նստած գիտտերն իրենց կ՚ընդլայնին՝
Ու կը խմեն Հեշտութիւնն իրենց տակէն սաՀող ջրին։
Ուսի թասերը աՀա քարերուն վրայ կը Հայչեն,
Յօտտՙխ թասերն, որոնք մերթ սիրտերու պէս կը ճայթին՝
Այդ անպատում մերկութեանց ծառայելու ժամանակ։
Կը քրքրրի կաևն աՀա, ձօթրինաբոյր կաևը գով,
Ծաղկաճիւթով գանգուած՝ գոր մեր նախնիք կ՚ուտէին,
Մազերն անով կը ձեփուին, ու կը դառնան ապրշում,
Լանջքերն անով կ՚օձանուին, ու կ՚ըլլան նման փրփուրի.
Անոր խիստովը պաղուկ, եւ լցրծուն շաղախով
Կը գովանան Հուրիներն, որովայնին կը լցկեն
Գետի խիձին պէս ողորկ ու թաւշօրէն օձանուտ։
Կ՚եռան ջուրերն, կը լուան կրրակներն այդ պաչտելի.
Կը փրփրին օձանները՝ Մաքրութիւններն անգամ մ՚ալ
Իրենց մածան լոյսերուն մէջ մաքրելու ի խնդիր։
Ջուրն, որ ամէն կողմանէ, պորտաքարին շուրջն ի վար,
Կ՚Հոսի կ՚երթայ՝ կոյուղին իսկ բուրումով լեցնելու,
Գո՛րշ է կաևով ու կիրով, լեղի կիրով Հերաթափ,
Եւ իր ուխին Հետ մէկտեղ մերթ կը դլձ կը տանի

Navelstones. Their hair, they comb their long,
Long hair endlessly down to the tips
With gold-covered combs, while their fingers
Glitter with the sparkle of their diamond rings.
The houris sometimes feel listless and faint,
And sometimes shiver suddenly when, from
The high vaporous dome above, some cold,
Fresh dew falls straight between their breasts.
Behold! the marble founts, the thousand taps
Now bursting one on the other
Tumultuously, as ashen vapors
Rise toward the dome, rise sinuously and slow;
The water overflows on every side
And winds its way to the empty water troughs.
Houris at their baths! Canova's graces
They all seem to be, and as closely twined,
Gathered round the sparkling marble basins.
They bathe their breasts, their curving limbs and arms,
All their lovely flesh;
And, seated on the navelstones, their thighs
Spread, spread and taste the delightful
Water which glides by and titillates.
Behold! the golden dippers ring across
The stones; the boxwood dippers sometimes break,
Like hearts, in the hands of these lovely nudes;
The argil-cool, thyme-scented clay dissolves
As they stroke it through their flowing waves of hair,
Transforming them to silk; and the clay
Cleans and anoints their breasts, hiding them in foam;
And, with the coolness of the argil's foam,
Its slippery substance, the houris grow refreshed,
They rub their bellies smooth,
Gleaming as sand on a whitened beach.
The water foams and washes pure
These beautiful maidens of Oriental fire.
And now from every side of the navelstones
The water flows down and away,
Rushing away, toward sewer troughs,
And giving even to these a delicate, perfumed scent.
The water is grey, with lime and argil,
And, as it swells, it carries along

Թխակուտակ թնճուկներ, անութներու գանգուրներ,
Եւ խոփներն ադումած այդ կիպերեան լուսեղէն
Արձաններուն կենեղուտ՝ որոնք այլեւս ուժաթափ
Կը լեցընեն Հուսկ թասերն, թասերը Հուսկ կը պարպեն.
Գուրեն Հե՛ղ մ՚ալ կը յորդին, բաղնիքն Հեղ մ՚ալ կ՚ադմկի,
Ջուրն եեփուն կը վազէ, Հե՛ղ մ՚ալ կ՚լողան Հուրիներն.
Կը բուրկի մորթերնին վարդի մը պէս բոցավառ.
Եւ նուաղուն բիբերով, թասերն՝ իրենց գլուխին,
Կուրձքերնուն վրայ միշտ գրկած դզգերն իրենց ծիծերուն՝
Այլեւս դուրս կը փութան, չարան չարան, Հեւասպառ,
Անդայտացած շոգիով, կակաչներու պէս բոսոր...
Օ՛, գանգուրներն յորդառատ՝ իրենց կուրձքին վրայ մերկ,
Օ՛, գանգուրները խսում, կաթիներով ծանրացած,
Որոնք բոբիկ ոտքերնուն՝ սատափ ցօղեր կը ծորեն...,
Ի՛նչպէս պատմել ձեր օծումն, ի՛նչպէս պատմել ձեր գարդերն՝
Երբ մարմիննիդ կը սրբէք, եւ կուրքի պէս կը Հագուիք...
Թող Համբուրեմ մա՛տերնիդ՝ դոր դուք այսօր կը թաթխէք
Հինաներու գուշին խորն՝ իբր արիւնոտ սրտի մէջ,
Թող Համբուրեմ մազերնիդ՝ կնդրուկներով օժանուտ՝
Որոնք, գիշերը, լուսնին տակ, կը բուրեն բարձին վրայ,
Եւ յօնքերնիդ ծարուրուած, ամպասման թարթիչնիդ,
Եւ լա՛նչքը ձեր՝ որ փաղփուն մանեակներով ոսկեշար
Ամուսնական անկողնին նշողուն ջա՛Հը կ՚ըլլայ.
Թող Համբուրեմ պորտը ձեր՝ ուր ծրարած կը ծածկէք
Թէ՛ Արաբիոյ Հաշիշներն եւ թէ՛ մուշկերն Ափրիկեան։
Ձեր տուներն ա՛յժմ կ՚երթաք գոծարներով բեռնալոր...
Թո՛ղ սալարկները Քաղքին ձեր քայլերէն թարմանա՛ն...
Յուրտը խածնէ՛ թուլերնիդ, ուայտերնիդ բոսրէ՛.
Վարշամակէ՛ն ձեր տամուկ, քղանցքներէ՛ն ծփծփուն
Արտաբուրէ՛ եւ յորդի՛ լոգանքին Հոտը ծոթրին.
Եւ լեցընէ գռեՀներն, Հրապարա՛կն եւ ուղի՛ն.
Աւելցած մասն այն Հացին՝ դոր դուք բաղնիք կը տանիք,
Ձոր թասին մէջ կը դնէք, եւ կը ծածկէք դենձակով,

Small hairs from under their arms, brown twinings from
Hair, downy leavings from these pale, white
And living statues, who now fill
Their final dippers, slowly,
And slowly pour water down their backs.
The steaming water runs, once more the baths
Roar, the troughs are gorged once more,
Once more the houris bathe, and their skins take fire
Like flaming full-blown roses in the sun.
With languid eyes and the dippers raised high
They bathe clean their full, smooth breasts.
In the rare vapor, red as tulips,
Beauty on beauty, the houris leave the bath.
O the luxurious curls slanting onto their breasts,
O those wet curls heavy with water,
With drops that fall as pearls around
Their groomed and dimpled feet; to sing,
O just to sing of their charms and rare perfume,
The glow of their bodies, the sandals, silks, and veils!
Those fingers, that today dipped into
The depths of henna bowls, as into a bloody
Heart, let me just kiss them; and let me
Kiss that hair, silked with sweet oils,
Hair that in the night, beneath the moon,
Gives its scent to the down filled pillows;
O to kiss, to press against my lips
Their aromatic brows, their curving lashes,
Bosoms dazzling with brilliant jewels,
Whose stones illuminate as torches
Around the bridal bed—O but to press
My lips to their navels, where deeply concealed,
Rests Arabian hashish
And Afric musk! Now bound homeward, and burdened,
So prettily, with precious stones and rare jewels,
Lightly scented with oils and thyme
Whose fragrance clouds their paths,
The city squares, scents the leavings in
Luncheon baskets, and trails its perfumes deep
Inside the folds of undulating skirts—
Now bound homeward they go their different ways,
The cold slapping their cheeks red,

Թող արձակէ՛ բուրումն իր՝ տարաշխարհիկ համեմով,
Չի այն ատեն փողոցներն Արեւելեան Քաղաքին
Պիտի զգան թէ Մայիան Հետքերնուղ վրա՛յ կը ծաղկի,
Եւ թարմացած մայթերէն Գարո՛ւն, Գարո՛ւնը կ'անցնի։—

The pavement echoing the sound of their footfalls,
Perfumed footsteps on Orient streets;
And tracing footprints tender as flowers, as blooms
Of May, will make the streets themselves think
That spring, the soul of spring is passing by.

Միսաք Մեծարենց

Missak Metsarents

1885–1908

Հիւղը

Դաշտի ճամբու մը վրան,
կամ ստորոտը լերան,
ուղեւորին ժամանման
սպասող Հիւղն ըլլայի:
Ու զգուանքիս կանչէի
ես ճամբորդներն անժաման,
ու ճամբուն վրայ մենաւոր,
ու ճամբուն վրայ ոսկեման,
եկուորներուն դիմաւոր՝
ծխանիս ծուխն ամպէի:

Ու դրդանքիս կանչէի
ուղեւորներ պարտասուն
ու բարեւի մը փոխան
Հազար բարիք ես տայի.
Հազար բարիք ես տայի, —
գոլը կրակին ճարճատուն,
կութքը բերրի դաշտերուն,
բոլոր միրգերն աշունի,
ու մեղր, ու կաթ, ու գինի...

Ու լսէի ես ցայգուն,
քովը կրակին ճարճատուն՝
երգն իրիկուան եկուորին.
ու ջամբէի ես ցայգուն
երազներով պատառուն
նինջ՝ իրիկուան եկուորին:

Ու լսէի ես այգուն,
սրտասպատար ու տրոփուն
գովքն իրիկուան եկուորին.
ու դիտէի ես այգուն,
ու խոկայի օրն ի բուն
երթն իրիկուան եկուորին...:

Ու ձմեռներն ալ համբուն,
Հրաւիրակ զուարթուն,
կանգնէի քովը ճամբուն
ու ճիւնապատ Հէք մարդուն

The Hut

I wish I were a hut
On a road in some field,
Or a hut below some hill—
A wayside place for travelers
Alone on their way.
I wish I could call my concern
To the harried travelers,
And on the winding golden road
Make them welcome,
Smoke billowing from my chimney.

I wish I could give comfort
To weary travelers,
And in exchange for their greeting
Do them a thousand kind turns.
Yes, do a thousand good turns,
The fire logs crackling,
The crop of the fertile fields,
All the fruits of autumn
And milk and honey and wine.

I wish I might listen till daybreak
To their praise of the fire,
The song of the traveler at evening,
And, asleep, wrapped in dreams,
I wish I could send off at daybreak
The nightfall comer.

And I wish I might hear at daybreak,
Cordial and happy,
The praise of one who comes at nightfall,
And, at daybreak, see
And wonder all through the night
About the departure of the one who comes at evening.

And patiently all through winter, too,
I wish I might stand along the roadside
With my arms outstretched wide
And in the stance of a beaming beckoner,
Offer with warmth and ready cheer

Ես Հայրօրէն, լայնաբաց
երկու թեւրս պարզեմ․
մի՛շտ քաղցրագին, նիւթացած
Հրաւէ՛րն ես լլայի։

Ա՛հ, լլայի՛, լլայի՛,
դաշտի ճամբու մը վրան
կամ ստորոտը լերան,
ուղեւորին ժամանման
սպասող Հի՛ւղն լլայի։

My fatherly invitation to a frostbitten traveler—
I wish I could always be taken for
The one who beckons travelers to his door.

Oh, if only I could be, could ever be
On a road in some place,
At the foot of some hill,
So that for those who travel
I could be the waiting hut.

Ռուբէն Սեւակ
Rouben Sevak
1885–1915

Ինչո՞ւ

Ինչո՞ւ, ինչո՞ւ զիս սիրեցիր,
Փոքրիկ աղջիկ, քեզի մե՛ղք էր.
Փոքրիկ ծոցիդ թիթե՛ռ պէտք էր.
Դուն ձեր արձի՛ւ մը բանտեցիր...

Կապոյտ աչուիդ երբ որ բացիր,
Կապո՛յտ աղջիկ՝ պլպլուն ե՛րդ էր.
Քե՛զ ալ սիրոյ մրմո՛ւնչ պէտք էր,
Դուն գուժկան մռո՛ւնչրս ընտրեցիր...

Ես կ'երթա՛մ մի՛շտ, անձայրածի՛ր
Դամբաններ են ոտքիս Հետքե՛րը,
Քեզ սիրոյ մեղմ սի՛րք մը պէտք էր,
Դուն փոթորկի՛ն կուրծքդ բացիր...

Կ'այրի՛ն աչերրդ սեւածիր,
Պիտի մեռնի՛ս, այդպէս մ'ե՛րդեր,
Քեզի փոքրիկ աճը մը պէտք էր,
Դուն Սէր-Աստուա՛ծը սիրեցիր...

Why?

Why, why did you fall in love with me?
Pity on you, little girl,
Your little heart is a size for a butterfly,
But you've imprisoned an ancient eagle there . . .

When you opened your blue eyes,
Blue girl, a bulbul's song was there;
You needed to hear a whisper of love,
You listened to my baleful groan.

I'm always wandering, the traces
Of my feet go past endless tombs;
You needed soft love to cover your heart,
But you bared it to the storm . . .

Your eyes are dark with a certain fire,
Don't sing in that way, or you'll surely die;
You needed to love a little love,
You loved the very Love-god himself . . .

Achvit (eyes) and *aghching* (girl) are near rhymes in Armenian; the poet here plays on words when he writes *blue girl*.

Վահան Տէրեան

Vahan Derian

1885–1920

Լուսաբացին նա բարձրացաւ կախաղան

Լուսաբացին նա բարձրացաւ կախաղան...
(Արեւածագ, օ՜, արշալոյս արիւնոտ),
Կանգնած էին գինուորներն ու քահանան,
Գունատ ու լուռ կանգնած էին նրա մօտ...

Ճեր քահանան ո՛չ մի աղօթք չէր յիշում...
(Սիրտը նրա շշնջում էր՝ անիծի՛ր),
Լուսածագի ծիրանավառ մշուշում,
Ցայտում էին ճաճանչները ցան ու ցիր...

Մռայլ սպան լուռ շրջում էր աչ ու ճախ...
(Արդեօք յիշե՞ց նա իր մօրը Հեռաւոր),
Գունատում էր սեւ գիշերը եւ ուրախ
Արեգակն էր ոսկեզօծում սար ու ձոր...

Լուսաբացին նա բարձրացաւ կախաղան...
(Արեւածագ, օ՜, արշալոյս արիւնոտ),
Կանգնած էին գինուորներն ու քահանան,
Գունատ ու լուռ կանգնած էին նրա մօտ...

Աշուղի Միջից

Աշուղի միջից, — տեսի՛լ դիւթական, —
Բացւում է կրկին նայիրին տրտում.
Ո՞ր երկրի սրտում թախիծ կայ այնքան,
Եւ այնքան ներում — ո՞ր երկրի սրտում...
Որտե՞ղ են քարերն այնպէս վերամբարձ
Ձեռների նման պարզուած երկնքին,
Որտե՞ղ է աղօթքն այնպէս վեճ ու պարզ
Եւ գոհաբերումն այնպէս խնդագին...
Որտե՞ղ է խոցում այնպէս ճա՛ր ու խոր
Սի՛րտը մարդկային դաշոյնը քինոտ.
Որտե՞ղ է հոգին այնպէս վիրաւոր,
Եւ անպարտ երկիրն այնպէ՛ս արիւնոտ...

The Gallows

At daybreak he walked up the gallows
—Sunrise, O bloodied dawn—
The priest and soldiers waited there,
They stood pale and silent beside him . . .

The old priest did not remember a single prayer,
His heart was dark with curses,
In the grey fog of dawn
The sunrays scattered aimlessly . . .

The officer shifted left foot to right—
Did he remember his distant mother?
The black night began to pale, then take color,
The sun began to gild the hills and valleys . . .

At dawn he walked up the gallows
—Sunrise, O bloodied dawn—
The priest and soldiers waited there,
They stood pale and silent beside him . . .

In the Mist

In the mist of this present scene
There looms again the Nairean grief,
What other country carries such grief in its heart
And such forgiveness—what other country?
Where else are thrusting rocks
Bared like hands reaching to the sky?
Where else is prayer this true and plain
And where so willing the oblation?
Where does the vengeful dagger lie, that stabs
As wickedly, deeply, into a heart?
Where else is the soul so wounded,
And the innocent earth so bloody?

Nairean is an adjectival form of Nairi, the ancient Armenian name for Armenia.

Հրաժեշտի Գազել

Ամէն վայրկեան սիրով տրտում՝ ասում եմ ես մնաս բարով.
Բո՛րբ արեւին իմ բոց սրտում ասում եմ ես մնաս բարով:

Մնաք բարով, ասում եմ ես, բոլոր մարդկանց՝ չար ու բարի,
Տանջուղող ու որբ Ադամորդուն՝ ասում եմ ես մնաս բարով:

Մնաք բարով, ասում եմ ես, ընկերներիս՝ մօտ ու Հեռու,
Ոստխներիս՝ չար ու արթուն, ասում եմ ես մնաք բարով:

Երկնի մովին, կանաչ ծովին, անտառներին խոր ու մթին,
Գարնան ամպին լոյս ողորտում, ասում եմ ես մնաք բարով:

Ուկեղծթայ իմ յուշերին, իմ գիշերին, իմ փշերին,
Արտոյտներին ոսկի արտում, ասում եմ ես մնաք բարով:

Ծաղիկներին դեռ չբացուած, դեռ չկիզուած հոգիներին,
Մանուկներին վառ-խլրտուն, ասում եմ ես մնաք բարով:

Գնում եմ ես մի մութ աշխարհ, Հեռու երկիր, էլ չե՛մ դալու,
Բարի՛ յիշէք ինձ ձեր սրտում, մնաք բարո՛վ, մնաք բարո՛վ:

Farewell Song

Every moment with sorrowing love I say farewell,
I say farewell to the sun, blazing in my heart.

I say goodbye to men everywhere, evil and kind,
I say goodbye to Adam's afflicted and orphaned sons.

Farewell to my close and distant friends,
Farewell to the enemies who watch me.

To the sky's blue, the sea's living green, the forest darkness,
To the light inside a spring cloud, I bid farewell.

To the shining chain of my memory, my nights and my pain,
To the larks in golden fields, I say farewell.

And goodbye to the unopened flowers, to the souls yet unkindled,
To the lively, playing children, farewell.

I am going to a darker earth, a remote land, I will not come back,
Remember me well in your hearts, I say goodbye, farewell.

Ազատ Վշտունի
Azad Veshtouni
1894–1958

Փոքրիկ Լրագրավաճառը

Խարտեաշ մազերով տղայ, լճակ աչքերո՛վ տղայ,
Հազում ես, ցո՛լրտ է սաստիկ, թշուա՛ռ, կը մեռնես հազէդ։
Տոկուն, համարձա՛կ տղայ, եռուն փողոցի՛ տղայ,
Վազի՛ր ու կանչիր ուժգին — նոր լո՛ւր, Հեռագի՛ր, գազե՛թ։

Բոպիկ ոտներով տղայ, առոյգ, կիսամե՛րկ տղայ,
Արագ թռչում ես մայթով, թնդում է մայթը վազէդ․
Հապա՛րպ, աշխատո՛դ տղայ, մրի, գրկանքի՛ տղայ,
Թռի՛ր, անցորդին կանչիր — նոր լո՛ւր, Հեռագի՛ր, գազե՛թ։

Սիրո՛ւն, սրիկա՛յ տղայ, անտուն, շրջմոլի՛կ տղայ,
Ամէնքը սիրում են քեզ, դիւթուած մանկական նազէդ։
Խայթող ու Հեգնո՛դ տղայ, գզրանք անսարգո՛դ տղայ,
Սուրա՛, բարձրաձայն կանչիր—նոր լո՛ւր, Հեռագի՛ր, գազե՛թ։

Փոքրիկ, տաս տարու տղայ, լմբոստ, մաքառո՛դ տղայ,
Հոսում է քրտինք ճակտէդ, այտէդ ու փոշոտ մազէդ։
Ցօղնած ու նիրհո՛դ տղայ, անկին կուշ եկա՛ծ տղայ,
Քնի՛ր փողոցում, կանչի՛ր — ցո՛լրտ է, մրսո՛ւմ եմ, գազե՛թ։

The Newsboy

You small, fair boy with your eyes like lakes,
Wretched boy, you're coughing, the air chills to cold and you will die
                                                                    of coughing.
You feisty tough boy of the crowded streets,
Run along now and shout out, "Late news, telegrams, paper!"

Barefoot boy, twirling, ragged boy,
You dash between flags and the pavement thuds beneath your feet;
You hustling, proud boy of soot and privation,
Fly, cry out to passersby, "Late news, telegrams, paper!"

You handsome, mischievous thing, you wandering, homeless boy,
All are taken with your boyish features, all love you;
You taunting, stinging boy, boy defying caress,
Run now, call out, "Late news, telegrams, paper!"

You, little boy, you ten years of stubborness, ten-year old, struggling
                                                                             boy,
Sweat is rolling down your face, your cheeks and dusty hair.
Thin boy, tired boy huddled in a corner,
You sleep on the hard street and cry, "It's cold, I'm cold, paper!"

Մատթէոս Զարիֆեան
Matevos Zarifian
1894–1924

Կարեկցութիւն

Պզտիկ աղջիկ մ՛ինծի կ՛ըսէ
Որ գիս խենթի պէս կը սիրէ.
Պզտիկ աղջիկ մը գիս սիրէ՛...

Գիշերն անհուն իմ աչքերուն
Երեւի դեռ նա չէ՛ տեսեր.
Պզտիկ աղջիկ մ՛ինծի տայ սէ՛ր...

Երեւի դեռ նա չէ՛ նայեր
Հոգւոյս խաւար անդունդին ի վար.
Պզտիկ աղջիկ մ՛ինձ սիրահա՛ր...

Եթէ լսէր թէ ո՛չ մէկ սէր
Այդ անդունդին մէջ կը շնչէր՝
Հէք պզտիկը չէ՞ր հառաչեր...

Ուստի եղբօր մը պէս ըսի
Որ լուսնին տակ մարդ կը մսի.
«Գնա՛, գնա՛, ննջէ՛», ըսի.

Ցեւող գացի՝ հեռուն լացի...

Compassion

A young girl tells me
She's deeply in love with me;
A young girl loves me . . .

It seems she hasn't yet seen
The depths of my eyes at night;
A young girl tenders her love to me . . .

It seems she hasn't yet looked
Into my soul's dark abyss;
A young girl loves me . . .

Could she but know not one love
Ever breathed in that place,
Wouldn't the poor little one sigh?

Hence, like a brother I told her
A body can catch cold under the moon;
"Go," I said, "and get to sleep."

Then I went far away and wept.

Եղիշէ Չարենց
Yeghishe Charents
1897–1937

Ես իմ անուշ...

Ես իմ անուշ Հայաստանի արևահամ բա'ռն եմ սիրում,
Մեր հին սազի ողբանուագ, լացակումած լա'րն եմ սիրում,
Արնանման ծաղիկների ու վարդերի բո'յրը վառման,
Ու նայիրեան աղջիկների հեզաճկուն պա'րն եմ սիրում:

Սիրում եմ մեր երկինքը մուգ, ջրերը ջինջ, լի'ճը լուսե,
Արևն ամռան ու ձմեռուայ վիշապաձայն բո'լքը վսեմ,
Մթում կորած խրճիթների անհիւրընկալ պատե'րը սև
Ու հնամեայ քաղաքների հազարամեայ քա'րն եմ սիրում:

Ո'ւր էլ լինեմ չե'մ մոռանայ ես ողբաձայն երգերը մեր,
Չե'մ մոռանայ աղօթք դարձած երկաթագիր գրքերը մեր —
Ինչքան էլ սո'ւր սիրտս խոցեն արիւնքամ վէրքերը մեր,
Էլի ես ո'րբ ու արնավառ իմ Հայաստան-եա'րն եմ սիրում:

Իմ կարօտած սրտի համար ո'չ մի ուրիշ հեքեաթ չկայ.
Նարեկացու, Քուչակի պէս լուսապսակ ճակատ չկայ.
Աշխա'րհ անցիր, Արարատի նման ճերմակ գագա'թ չկայ.
Ինչպէս անհաս փառքի ճամբայ՝ ես իմ Մասիս սա'րն եմ սիրում:

Հայրենիքում

Ձիւնապատ լեռներ ու կապոյտ լճեր:
Երկինքներ, որպէս երազներ հոգու:
Երկինքներ, որպէս մանկական աչեր:
Մենակ էի ես: Ինձ հետ էիր դու:

Երբ լսում էի մրմունջը լճի
Ու նայում էի թափանցիկ հեռուն —
Ճարթնում էր իմ մէջ քո սուրբ անուշչի
Կարօտը այն հին, աստղային, անհուն:

Sun-flavored Speech

I love my sweet Armenia's sun-flavored speech,
I love the plaintive musings of our ancient saz,
The crimson flowers, the burning fragrance of roses,
And the tender-bodied dance of the Nairean girls I love.

I love our evening dark sky, the transparent water, the flashing lake,
The summer sun, and the winter's dragon hissing a grand blizzard,
The forbidding black walls of huts, lost in the night,
And the stones of a thousand years and ancient towns.

Wherever I may be, I won't forget our songs of sorrow,
Nor forget our metal-graved books, now prayers to us,
However deeply our bloody suffering probes my heart,
I shall yet love my wounded, orphaned sweet Armenia.

My heart shall long to know no other tale:
Naregatsi, Kouchag—who now possesses their haloed brows?
Roam round the world, you'll not find a peak white as Ararat;
As the path of glory is endless, so is my love for the Massis mountain.

Metal-graved books. The passage refers to books in metal covers which are engraved with biblical scenes; several hundred of these books are preserved in the manuscript library at Yerevan, Armenia. They are part of the Armenian heritage and, hence, are "now prayers to us."
Kouchag and *Naregatsi* are much revered Armenian poets.

Fatherland

Snow-wrapped mountains and blue lakes,
Skies like dreams of the soul,
Skies like children's eyes.
I was alone. You were with me.

When I heard the whispers of the lake,
And looked unceasingly into the distance,
There rose in me that old longing
For you, that dream, holy, star-filled, infinite.

Կանչում էր, կանչում ճիւոտ լեռներում
Մէկը կարօտի իրիկնամուտին։
Իսկ դիչերն իջնում, ծածկում էր հեռուն,
Խառնելով հոգիս աստղային մութին․․․

Մահուան Տեսիլ

Որքա՜ն նման է եղել պահն այդ՝ մարող կանթեղի․․․
․ ․ ․ ․ ․ ․ ․ ․ ․ ․ ․ ․ ․ ․ ․
․․․ Նրա կոպերը երեք երբ քարացել են խաղաղ,
Կապոյտ բոցով բռնկուած վերջին ջերմում ուղեղի,
Նա տեսել է երեւի արեւային մի քաղաք․․․
Ինչպէս մաքուր մարմարի կապոյտ կողին նկարած
Արեւային ժամացոյց՝ քարոտեզն աճա քաղաքի, —
Պողոտաներ, փողոցներ՝ բոլորածիզ երկարած,
Իսկ կենտրոնում երկնահաս, գրանիտեայ մի բագին։
Ակնթարթում մի վեմ, որ երկարում է դարեր,
Փողփողում են ուղեզում, — սիրտ պայթելու չափ պայծառ, —
Սիւնաշարքեր, տեռասներ, աստիճաններ մարմարէ,
Եւ պարտէզներ ոսկեզօծ, շատրուանններ երգաճայն․․․
Աշտարակներ երկնահաս եւ կամարներ կորանիստ,
Թանդակազօծ կարնիզներ, պատուհաններ նուրբ հատած,
Եւ մարմարիոն մարմնագոյն, եւ գանգրահեր գրանիտ
Եւ վարդաբոյր տուֆաքար եւ բիլ բազալտ սրբատաշ․․․
․ ․ ․ ․ ․ ․ ․ ․ ․ ․ ․ ․ ․ ․ ․
Պարզել է ճեղքը դողդող դժպի ցնորքն այդ կապոյտ,
Այնքան մօտ է, այնքան մօ՛տ, — կը շօշափի նա հիմա, —
Բայց ծանրացել է յանկարծ ճեղքն հանճարեղ ու հմուտ,
Ընկել է վար՝ չոր կրծքին․․․ Լռութիւն։ Մահ։

In the clear evocative sunset
I called, called to the snow covered mountains;
Night fell, darkening the distance,
Mingling my soul with the starry dark.

A Vision of Death

How that moment was like a dying icon lamp
. . . .
. . . When his old lids turned to hard stone, peaceful;
In the brain's last warmth, caught in that blue flame,
He must have seen perhaps a sunny city . . .
Like a sundial painted on a blue facet of clean marble,
Oh, the map of that city—
Boulevards, and streets extending away,
And in the center a granite altar towering high.
In a moment's blink, a blink stretching into centuries,
There glitters in the brain, bright enough to burst the heart
—Colonnades, terraces, marble steps,
Gilded gardens, fountains singing like human voices . . .
Towers reaching the sky and bow-shaped arches,
Sculpted cornices, windows elaborately wrought,
Marble the color of flesh, and frizzly granite,
And rosy tufa stone, and basalt reverently hewn . . .
. . . .
His tremulous hand is stretched now to that blue phantom flame,
So close it is, so near—now touching—
But suddenly his great and skillful hand turns heavy,
Falls on his deserted breast . . . Silence. Death.

Նայիրի Զարեան

Nairi Zarian

1900–1969

Հայրենի Տուն

Այս գիշեր տեսայ մի անուշ երազ.
Ես Հայրենի տունն էի նորոգում,
Մանկութեան երկինքն էր բացուել վրաս
Եւ արշալոյսներ կային իմ հոգում։

Այնտեղ էր մայրս, Հայեացքը պայծառ,
Մայրենի լեզուով խօսում էր առուն.
Խշում էր բակում Հինաւուրց մի ծառ...
Այնպէս ծանօթ էր եւ այնպէս գարուն...

Երդիկից կախած չողն արեգական
Թւում էր Հոգուս ոսկեայ բանալի,
Արեւն էր նայում աչքով մայրական,
Եւ քաղցր էր աշխարհն ու Հասկնալի...

To my Native Home

Tonight I had a sweet dream:
I was rebuilding the home of my childhood,
The sky of my childhood spread over my head,
And rising dawns shed color in my soul.

My mother was there, her face glowed bright,
The stream chattered away in my native tongue,
An ancient tree stirred in the yard—
It was all so familiar, all so like spring.

The sunbeam that slid from the rooftop
Seemed to be my soul's golden key;
The sun looked down with a motherly warmth,
The world was sweet and knowable.

Սարմէն

Sarmen

1902–

Գառնուկը

Ցնծո՛ւմ, թնդո՛ւմ էր անտառը, անտառում կար կերուխում,
Չխնափրփուր հացն էր բուրում, կարմիր գինին ծիծաղում,
Շուրջպար բռնած ճոճւում էին աղջիկ, տղայ, մայր, մանուկ,
Մառին կապուած՝ պարն էր դիտում մտամոլոր մի գառնուկ։
Ես հովասուն հովիտն իջայ, որ աղբիւրը համբուրեմ
Եւ իմ ծարաւ մանկան համար սարի զուլալ ջուր բերեմ։
Վերադարձայ... խորովածի բոյրն էր բռնել սար ու քար,
Բաժակների երգն էր գնդում... բայց, ա՛խ, գառնուկը չկար։

The Lamb

The woodland shook, it thundered with laughter,
The white bread was fragrant, the red wine flowing,
Boy and girl and mother and child swayed in a circle dance.
A lamb tied to a tree
Pensively watched the dance.
I went down to the icy spring to wet my lips
And fetch some water for my thirsting child.
I returned . . . the aroma of shish kebab spread through the hills and valleys
And the song of glasses rang out—ah, but the lamb was no longer there.

Գեղամ Սարեան

Guegham Sarian

1902–1976

Բաժակը

Այս բաժակն անշուշտ, որ լուռ նայում էր ինձ,
Մերթ ուրախ է լինում, ու մերթ տխրաթախիծ,
Նրա մէջ վառ գինին՝ մերթ իբրև խնդութիւն,
Եւ մերթ տխրութեան պէս նայում է իմ հոգուն։

Եւ իմ սրտն էլ այդպէս մի բաժակի նման
Լցւում է մերթ խինդով, մերթ վշտով անսահման,
Վշտով լեցուն պահին՝ դարձեալ ուրախ եմ ես,
Որ չի՛ լինում սիրտս դատարկ բաժակի պէս։

The Glass

This lifeless glass winks at me,
Now turns joyous, now seems sad;
In it the purple wine, now like mirth,
Now like gloom, peers into my soul.

And my heart is also like a glass,
Now it fills with joy and now with gloom;
But when it fills with gloom, I am glad again
That my heart is not an empty glass.

Գուրգէն Մահարի

Gourgen Mahari
1903–1969

Գիշերը

Ողջ գիշեր բարդիները
Խշշացին չափարի մոտ,
Ողջ գիշեր ականջում էր
Իմ սիրտը այդ ձայներին.
Ինչ կանչում էր ողջ գիշեր
Հնօրեայ, հի՛ն մի կարօտ,
Կարկաչում էր մի անուն
Դաշտերից ու լայներից։

Մանձղաներ էին ցնծում,
Բամբիռներ արծաթաձայն,
Ողջ գիշեր հովը պարեց
Ա՛խ, այնքա՛ն, այնքա՛ն թեթեւ.
Ողջ գիշեր բռնել էի
Հնօրեայ, հին մի կածան,
Ու շուրջս մեռած օրեր,
Ու մեռած ծաղկեթերթեր...

Ձեր երգը ի՛մն է նորից,
Ու հիմա, երբ գիշեր է,
Ուղում է կարօտս խենթ
Ձրերի նման գարնան.
Ու այնպէս դեռ հեռու՛ է
Ինձ թւում է աղունը
Եւ օրերս թեւում են
Թեթեւ դե՛ռ ու դեռ վառման։

Ձեզ հետ եմ նորից աճում,
Բարտիներ, ճերմակ հարսներ,
Ցնորք իմ ոսկեհանդերձ,
Երկրային անգի՛ն համայք, —
Ես քո բերքն եմ ընդունել,
Քեզնով է ե՛րգն իմ հասել,
Իմ երկրի վառմա՛ն արեւ,
Նայիրեան ոսկէ՛ քնար...

Night

The whole night through the poplars
Rustled near the fence,
The whole night through my heart
Listened to the sound,
Nightlong there brushed softly past my ear
An old longing of long ago,
It trilled a name
Far and away across the fields.

Cymbals were set tinkling
And silver-sounding bandoras,
Ah, lightly, ever so lightly
The winds danced the whole night through;
The whole night through I held my way
Along a timeworn lane of long ago,
And dead days all around me
And the petals of dead flowers.

Your songs are mine once again
And now, when the nighttide is upon me,
My tumble of desires rushes again
Like the rising springtime streams,
And so it is my autumn days
Seem to me still remote,
And my days appear to me
Carefree still and brightly aflame.

I grow again with you,
O poplars, my white brides,
My dream's golden fabric,
Heaven's priceless charm—
My fruits have ripened beneath you,
From you my crops have come,
In the burning sun of my native land,
O golden Nairean lyre.

Վաղարշակ Նորենց

Vagharshak Norents

1903–1973

Քույրս

Ունի մի դեմք՝ ասես լուսին՝
Շուրջը երկու ամպ-խոպոպիկ․
Վարսերի հետ սափորն ուսին՝
Գնում է նա ոտաբոպիկ։

Ժպիտ ունի յոնքերի տակ, —
Ամպի տակի շողն է հրէ, —
Ինքն էլ այնքան նո՛րբք է, յստակ,
Որ տեսնում ես իր մէջ իրեն։

Աղբիւրի մոտ լուռ կանգնած՝
Նայում է նա ջրին այն ջինջ,
Նախ ժպտում է, ապա յանկարծ
Խառնում ջրին, ծիծաղ ու ճիչ․․․

Ու փրփրում են ծիծաղ ու ջուր․․․
Հրա՛շք, ինքն էլ քողուեց ամպով,
Դարձաւ ճերմակ-ճերմակ փրփուր․․․
Ափին մնաց դատարկ սափոր։

Sister

She has a face, shall it be said, like the moon,
Set among clouds of curls,
She goes forth barefoot,
Her hair slanting onto the jug on her shoulder.

Beneath her brows a smile sparks—
The beams beneath her lashes take on fire,
She is her self, so delicate, so distinctly
You see her very self in her.

She stands silent near the fountain,
She looks on the gleaming water,
She smiles, and then suddenly
The water mingles with her joy and laughter,

Laughter and water foaming together,
She is wondrous, veiled in clouds of spray,
She becomes a vision foaming white on white—
The empty jug in her hand still.

Սողոմոն Տարոնցի
Soghomon Taronsti
1904–1971

Մեր Արագիլը

Թխպոտ երկնով այսօր վերջին երամն անցավ,
Ձուեց հեռուն, տրտմաթախի՛ծ ու տարագիր։
Դու չե՛ս հասնի այդ երամին՝ հոգմահալած ու ցիրուցան,
— Դու կը մեռնե՛ս, ծեր արագիլ։

Երամն անցավ, վերջին անգամ, կղկղալեն սրտակեղեք,
Ու լսում էր վերջին երգը — անսփոփ ու անկարեկիր,
Քո թեւերը կոտրուել են որպես ցողուն, որպես եղեգ,
— Դու կը մեռնե՛ս, ծեր արագիլ։

Քո հին բույնը բզկտում է անգութ քամին մեր դաշտերի,
Ծանծաղուտի վրայ նա չէ՞ր, որ պարեց խոլ ու ցալագին։
Քո աչքերում նուազում է կապոյտ երազը շամբերի,
— Դու կը մեռնե՛ս, ծեր արագիլ։

Ա՛խ, տեսնում եմ, դրել ես դու մարգարիտէ կտուցը քո
Կոտրուած, թոյլ թեւերիդ տակ, սպասելով վերջին երգին։
Երազներիդ երամները լուռ՝ մարում են վերջին երգով,
— Դու կը մեռնե՛ս, ծեր արագիլ։

Երամն անցավ թխպոտ երկնով, ու չնայե՛ց երբեք հետև,
Ու թողեց որ՝ դու լուռ մեռնես մենա՛կ, տրտո՛ւմ ու տարագիր,
Միայն քամին ծառերի հետ շշնջաց քո սուգը թեթև,
— Որ դու մեռա՛ր, ծեր արագիլ։

Old Stork

Today the flock passed through the heavy sky for the last time,
Traveled away and far; exiled and burdened with sorrow,
You will not be reaching that scattered and wind-driven flock
—Old stork, you are about to die.

With heart-splitting screams, the flock passed over, the last time,
Its desolate cry was heard, all without pity;
Your wings are broken, like a stalk, like a cane
—Old stork, you are about to die.

The harsh plainwind tears this old nest of yours to shreds—
Wasn't it on the marsh that it soughed and wildly danced
As the blue vision of thickets slowly faded from your eyes?
—Old stork, you are about to die.

Ah, I see you have tucked your shining beak
Under your frail, broken wing, waiting for your last song.
The flocks of your dreams are still dying with the last song
—Old stork, you are about to die.

Across the heavy sky the flock passed, and never looked back,
Left you unclaimed, to die exiled alone, forlorn, silent,
Only the wind spoke your grief here, lightly among the trees
When you died, old stork, when you died.

Վահէ–Վահեան

Vahe Vahian

1908–

Հոգենուագ

Երբ ես մեռնիմ, վա՛րդ մը միայն՝ դագաղիս,
Մօրս հոգիին կարօտի ցօ՛ղը վրան...
Ճերմա՛կ ըլլայ... եւ գոյներու ո՛չ մէկ գիծ՝
Արիւնավառ վերջալոյսէ մը գարնան։

Ո՛չ զանգակներ եղերաձայն, ո՛չ նուագ․
Բարեկամներ միայն քալեն ինծի հետ․
Ցեղոյ, Հանդարտ, աւերակէ աւերակ,
Հոսի՛ հոգիս մռայցումին մէջ անհետ։

Ո՛չ շարական, ո՛չ խունկ ու մոմ, ո՛չ արցունք...
Անտառին մէջ պիտի հովերը նորէն
Երգեն իրենց հոգենուա՛գը խորունկ,
Պիտի նորէն ծռին լոյսե՛ր աստղերէն։

Պիտի երկիրն արթննայ միշտ իր ծիրէն,
Պիտի ծաղկի եղբեւանին Մայիսին,
Պիտի դարձեա՛լ գոչեր անցնին մայթերէն,
Ու ցնծատան մէջ փրկերէ՝ ցոփ գինին։

Ցոյսը նորէն պիտի քալէ ծովափէն,
Թաց աչքերով աղջրնակի մը նման,
Կամ գինովի մը պէս գոյարթ երգելէն,
Եւ առօրեան պիտի գտնէ՛ իր ճամբան։

Կեա՛նք, արեւէդ չառած կանխեց մ՚իսկ բաժին,
Պիտի շրջիմ ես մութին մէջ անվախճան,
Ինծի հետ լոկ վի՛շտը մեռած երազին,
Եւ յիշատակն՝ անկարելի ապաստան։

Requiem

Only a rose on my bier when I die,
The dear dew of my mother's hope upon it,
Let it be white, no shadow of color
Taken from a bloodshot, twilit spring.

No mourning bells, no music,
Only friends to walk with me
Then, peacefully, from ruin to ruin,
My soul will glide into traceless oblivion.

No hymns, no incense, no candles, no tears,
In the forest, again, the winds
Will sing their deep requiem,
And light will flow down again from the stars.

The earth will circle always in its orbit,
The May lilac will bloom again,
Couples will stroll again along the sidewalks,
And lecherous wine will foam again in taverns.

Hope will be there along the seashore again,
Misty-eyed as a young girl,
Or singing out a cheerful song, like a drunk,
And ordinary life soon begins its day.

Life, before I share even a portion of your sacred fire,
I'll be roaming the boundless dark,
Only the pangs of my dead dreams with me
And the remembrance of an unreachable haven.

Սուրէն Վահունի

Souren Vahouni

1910–

Ծիծեռնակ

Հավքեր կան՝ մարդուց երկար են ապրում...
Եւ ծիծեռնակն այն, — որ ցուրտ աշերում
Հանդիպեց մի օր մեր պանդուխտ երգչին, —
Գուցէ չի երգել դեռ երգն իր վերջին։

Ճախրում է գուցէ, նորից ճուռոդում՝
Բոյն հիւսած երգչի երազած գիւղում,
Եւ աշտարակի բարդիները ճիգ
Լսում են նրա երգը գեղեցիկ։

Դեռ կ'ապրի՝ գուցէ... Նրան կը լսեն
Պոէտներ ուրիշ, որ մեզ պէս կ'ասեն,
Թէ ինչո՞ւ, ինչո՞ւ, երբ աշխարհ եկանք՝
Մեզ էլ չտրուեց այդքան երկար կեանք։

Եւ կը նախանձեն այդ նոյն ծիծառին,
Որ թառած գուցէ իմ տնկած ծառին,
Մեզնից յետոյ էլ դեռ պիտի երգի
Զքնաղ գարունները իմ հայրենիքի։

Swallow

There are birds that outlive men,
And that swallow, that on a cold shore
Met a wandering singer one day,
Perhaps has not yet sung its final song.

Perhaps it hovers once again, singing,
Its nest woven in the village of the poet's dream,
And the tall, straight poplars of Ashtarak
Still listen to the swallow's lovely song.

Perhaps it still lives on—and other
Poets, who hear it like us, will ask
Why, when we came into the world, why
Weren't we allowed a life as long?

And they shall envy that very same swallow
Who, perched perhaps on the tree I planted,
Will be singing still, after we're gone,
The beautiful spring of my fatherland.

Աշոտ Գրաշի

Ashod Grashi

1911–1973

Ա՛խ, Մինա Ընկաւ

Այսօր կարդացի Լէյլի-Մեջնունը,
Սիրոյ մրմուռը, ա՛խ, մինըս ընկաւ,
Ողջ գիշեր չեկաւ աչքերիս քունը,
Եարիս տան դուռը, ա՛խ, մինըս ընկաւ։

Նա Ղարաբաղի կոկոն մի վարդ էր,
Այնքան ուրախ էր, այնքան գուարթ էր,
Շրթունքներն էին կակաչի թերթեր,
Անուշ համբոյրը, ա՛խ, մինըս ընկաւ։

Հագի չորերը ալուան էր, ա՛լ էր,
Աստղաշող թշին ջուխտակ թուխ խալ էր,
Երբ ման էր գալիս, սարի մարալ էր,
Օրօր-չորօրը, ա՛խ, մինըս ընկաւ։

Զմրուխտ գարուն էր՝ եարիս գգուեցի,
Մազիկ քաղեցի, ծաղկով գուզեցի,
Մէկ էլ չիմացայ, թէ ո՞նց գրկեցի,
Գրկելու օրը, ա՛խ, մինըս ընկաւ։

Եա՛ր, կեանքըդ վարդի թաղերում անցաւ,
Խոտին նոր դրած չաղերում անցաւ,
Գոհար խաղողի բաղերում անցաւ,
Ձեր բաղի նուռը, ա՛խ, մինըս ընկաւ։

Դու մի նչենու անուշ նուշն էիր,
Թնքունեըից էլ դու քնքուշ էիր,
Սրտիս պարտէզում նախշուն դուշ էիր,
Քո խաս փետուրը, ա՛խ, մինըս ընկաւ։

Ես Հովիւ էի սարերի լանջում,
Ուկէ սրինգով եա՛ր էի կանչում,
Ձորն էիր իջնում, քո կուժը լցնում,
Այն պաղ աղբիւրը, ա՛խ, մինըս ընկաւ։

Դու գետի ափին բուսած մի եղէգ,
Ես կեանքում քեզ միշտ գերի՛ եմ եղել,
Քո յօնքերն էին կոռնկի թեւեր,
Աչքերիդ Հուրը, ա՛խ, մինըս ընկաւ։

Գիտեն ծառերը եւ ծաղիկները,
Երբ քեզ բաց արի ես սրտիս ախրը,

Ah, It Came to Mind

Today I read from Leyli-Mejnoun—
Ah, the grief of love came to mind;
I didn't sleep the whole night through—
Ah, my darling's threshold came to mind.

She was a budding rose of Karabagh,
So gay she was and ever so happy,
Her lips were full as tulip petals—
Ah, her sweet kisses came to mind.

The clothes she wore were all burgundy red,
On her star-bright cheeks stood a pair of moles,
Her gait was that of a slender mountain deer—
Ah, her swaying gait came to mind.

It was an emerald spring when I caressed my love,
I gathered flowers, and with garlands linked her to me,
I don't know how it happened—I suddenly held her—
Ah, the time I held her came to mind.

O darling your life passed in rosy realms,
On grass freshly touched with dew,
Among vineyards bearing gemlike grapes—
Ah, the pomegranates of your orchard came to mind.

You were the sweet kernel from my almond tree,
You were the daintiest of the dainty,
In the garden of my heart you were the bright-plumed bird—
Ah, your bright plumes came to mind.

I was a shepherd on the mountain slopes,
Often I called my love with my golden pipe,
She descended the gorge to fill her jug—
Ah, that cool spring came to mind.

You were a canebrake grown at the river's edge,
Your eyebrows were a crane's curved pair of wings,
All my life through I have been your slave—
Ah, the fire in your eyes came to mind.

The flowers and the trees both know
When it was I bared this heart of mine to you,

Ի՞նչ անէծք տուին քո հերն ու մերը,
Նրանց թուքն ու մուրը, ա՛խ, միտքս ընկաւ:

Այսօր կարդացի Լեյլի-Մեջնունը,
Սիրոյ մրմուրը, ա՛խ, միտքս ընկաւ...
Ողջ գիշեր չեկա՛ւ աչքերիս քունը,
Սիրուհուս դուռը, ա՛խ, միտքս ընկաւ:

Your father, mother placed a curse on me,
Ah, their spite and scorn came to mind.

Today I read from Leyli-Mejnoun—
Ah, the grief of love came to mind;
I didn't sleep the whole night through—
Ah, my darling's threshold came to mind.

Մուշեղ Իշխան

Moushegh Ishkhan

1913–

Դուն Միացար Մեր Հոգին

Մա՛յր իմ՝ արեւ ու Հեռանո՛ւչ լուսնկայ,
Դարձար նշխա՛ր ու միացար մեր հոգին,
Եւ հոդն անուշ հայրենիքին հնամեայ,
Քիչ մ՚աւելի՝ անուշցաւ...

    Մա՛յր իմ՝ երկինք եւ առաւօ՛տ սրբալոյս,
    Դուն մեր հոգին տուիր հոգիդ խնկաբոյր
    Եւ հոգը սուրբ՝ լուսապսակ պապերուս՝
    Քիչ մ՚աւելի՝ սրբացաւ...

Մա՛յր իմ, դուն գանձ եւ անսպա՛ռ ոսկեհանք,
Դարձար խորհուրդ եւ հոգակոյտ աննշան,
Բայց գանձն անխոցդ մեր հոգերու լանջքին տակ՝
Քիչ մ՚աւելի աճեցաւ...

    Մա՛յր իմ՝ աղբիւր անհաս հրաշքին,
    Գացիր ննջել Լուսաւորչի աստղին տակ
    Եւ սիրտն անհուն Հայաստանի մայր հոգին
    Քիչ մ՚աւելի՝ մայրացաւ...

Մա՛յր իմ՝ երդիկ, մա՛յր իմ՝ սեղա՛ն տոհմական,
Հարազատ բառ եւ սուրբ բառբա՛ռ մայրենի,
Քեզմով հիմա աշխարհն հայոց աննման
Քիչ մ՚աւելի՝ հայացաւ...

Joined with our Land

O my mother, sun and remote moon,
Transformed into communion bread, you joined with our land
And the age-old earth of our homeland, always sweet,
Became still sweeter.

> O my mother, lit by holy heaven and morning,
> You gave your soul, laden with incense, to our land,
> And the land of our honored fathers, always holy,
> Became more sacred still.

O my mother, treasure, inexhaustible gold mine,
You became both mystery and paltry mound of earth,
Yet the store of unfound treasure, lying deep in our earth,
Became still richer.

> O my mother, source of love's unreachable miracle,
> You went to your sleep beneath the Illuminator's star,
> And the boundless heart of Armenia's own earth
> Became still more motherly.

O my mother, O refuge, O reverenced altar,
Native language, holy vernacular,
Now with your presence, the peerless Armenian world
Became a little more Armenian.

Gregory, called the *Illuminator,* was an historical figure; he brought Christianity to Armenia in A.D. 301.

Յովհաննէս Շիրազ

Hovhanness Shiraz
1914–

Էքսպրոմտ

Մենք խաղաղ էինք մեր լեռների պես,
Դուք հողմերի պես խուժեցիք վայրագ։

Մենք ձեր դեմ ելանք մեր լեռների պես,
Դուք հողմերի պես ոռնացիք վայրագ։

Բայց մենք յաւե՛րժ ենք մեր լեռների պես,
Դուք հողմերի պես կը կործի՛ք վայրագ։

Նիագարա

Նիագարա՛, Նիագարա՛, կ՚իջնես ցած՝
Բարձունքներից յաւերժօրէն խոված։

Նիագարա՛, այս աշխարհում դառն ու ցուրտ,
Մայր բնութեան յաւերժական դու գայրոյթ։

Նիագարա՛, ինչքա՛ն դռաս, օ՛, կրկին
Անդունդներդ նե՛րդ են քո խոլ տարերքին։

Նիագարա՛, ես քո տարերքն սպիտակ՝
Երգի ժամին զգում եմ ի՛մ կրծքի տակ։

Սիրտս՝ Ալեւոր Կաղնու Մէջ Դրի

Սիրտս՝ ալեւոր կաղնու մէջ դրի,
Կռացած կաղնին նորի՛ց բողբոջեց,
Բարձրացաւ, կանգնեց ընդդէմ հողմերի,
Եւ ջահելացած՝ նորի՛ց հառաչեց։

Եւ մատաղ սիրտս՝ ճախրանքի ծարաւ,
Զառամեալ արծուի կրծքի տակ դրի,
Մեռնող արծիւը թե՛ւ առաւ, թռա՛ւ
Որսի հետեւից ջահել օրերի․․․

Impromptu

We were peaceful as our mountains,
You invaded like savage storms.

We rose against you like our mountains,
You howled like savage storms.

But we are eternal as our mountains,
You will die out like savage storms.

Niagara

Niagara, Niagara, you crash down
From great heights, everlastingly angry.

Niagara, eternal wrath of nature,
You are cold and bitter in this world.

Niagara, however much you roar, yet
The abyss is narrow for your seething.

Niagara, in my time of singing I feel
Your cloudy cataracts in my breast.

Oak and Eagle

I placed my heart inside an ancient oak;
The drooping oak greened again,
Towered high, stood against the wind,
And, restored to youth, rustled in contentment.

And my lovetorn heart, so eager to soar,
I put in the breast of a dying eagle;
The dying eagle spread wing and rose high,
To prey again as in the days of its youth.

Գուրգէն Բորեան

Gourgen Borian
1915–1971

Այս ճանապարհը Անվե՛րջ Լինէր

Այս ճանապարհը անվե՛րջ լինէր,
Ինչպէս ճամբան այն յարդագողի...
Զլինէ՛ր ցերեկ, լինէր գիշե՛ր,
Եւ անցնէինք մենք գաղտագողի։

Անցէինք մէկտեղ... եւ իրարու,
Ինչպէս աստղերը երկնում հեռու,
Շշնջայինք մենք սիրոյ խոսքե՛ր...
Այս ճանապարհը անվե՛րջ լինէր։

Չափէի՛նք մենք ուղին անցած,
Եւ չնայէի՛նք երբեք մենք ետ,
Չհարցնէինք՝ ո՞րքա՞ն մնաց...
Այս ճանապարհը անվե՛րջ լինէր։

Եւ այդ ճամբի պէս յար երջանիկ
Սիրոյ խորհուրդը լինէր անմե՛ռ,
Լինէր յաւե՛րժ ու... մենք քայլէի՛նք,
Եւ ճանապարհը անվե՛րջ լինէր...

This Endless Journey

O may this journey be endless
As the span of the Milky Way—
May there be night without day,
That we may journey in stealth.

Journey on, and near each other,
As the stars in the distant sky,
Whispering our words of love—
O may this journey be endless.

We shouldn't mind the traveled roads,
Nor should we ever look back,
We shouldn't ask how much is left—
O may this journey be endless.

And like that joy-lined road
Be the ancient secret of love
Everlasting, and—we keep walking on this earth—
O may this journey endless be.

Համո Սահեան

Hamo Sahian

1915–

Անտառում

Անտառում ամպի ծվէններ կային,．
Կապույտ մշուշներ կային անտառում．
Օրոր էր ասում աշունն անտառին,
Բայց դեռ անտառի քունը չէ'ր տանում։

Շշուկներ կային անտառում այնքան,
Եւ խոնաւ-խոնաւ բուրմունքներ կային...
Իրար փաթաթուած ստուէ'ր ու կածան,
Ու Հեռքե'ր, Հեռքե'ր, Հեռքե'ր մարդկային։

Եղեամն էր սունկի գլուխն արծաթում,
Մրսում էր կարծես վայրի նշենին,
Հանգստանում էր Հոզմը բացատում՝
Ականջն ամպրոպի ազդանշանին։

Եղնիկի հորթը մամուռը ծնշին,
Թոչում է իր մօր բառաչի վրայ,
Եւ որսականը թաց խոտերի միջին
Կորած Հետքերն էր որոնում նրա։

Փայտահատը Հին երգն էր իր կրկնում
Եւ տաք սղոցն իր իլղում էր կրկին,
Թեղին անտարբեր ականջ էր դնում
Տապալուած կաղնու խուլ Հառաչանքին։

Անտառապահի տնակի առաջ
Խարոյկն իր խաղաղ ծուխն էր ծածանում,
Եւ խարոյկի մօտ եղեւնին կանաչ
Սոճու Հետ սիրով գրոյց էր անում...

Անտառում խորին խորհուրդներ'ր կային
Եւ արձագանքներ կային անտառում...
Օրոր էր ասում աշունն անտառին,
Սակայն անտառի քունը չէր տանում։

In the Woods

There were small clouds in the woods,
Blue mist hung in the woods,
Autumn hummed softly in the woods,
But still the trees could not fall asleep.

There were whisperings in the woods,
And a richness of wet fragrance,
Shadows and lanes twined closely,
And traces, traces of men.

The dew silvered the mushroom caps,
The wild almond tree looked chill,
The wind came to rest in the glade,
Tilted to the sounds of thunder.

The deer calf, its muzzle moss-covered,
Leaps at its mother's cry,
And through the wet grass, the hunter
Seeks the lost trace of the deer.

The woodsman sings his old song again
And oils the warming saw again,
The breadfruit tree doesn't hear
The hushed sigh of the fallen oak.

Before the forest warden's hut
A bonfire gives up peaceful smoke,
And the green fir near the fire
Talks heartily with the cypress.

There were mysteries deep in the woods,
Echoes abounded in the woods,
Though autumn hummed softly in the woods,
The trees still could not fall asleep.

Նայիրեան Դալար Բարդի

Նազում ես ու շորորում գմբուխտէ քո շորերում,
Շուք արած ճամբու վրայ՝ մանկութեան կանա՛չ արտի,
Քո կանչը գնդո՛ւմ է գիլ իմ սրտի խոր ձորերում,
Իմ Հեռո՛ւ, Հեռո՛ւ, Հեռու՝ նայիրեան դալա՛ր բարդի։

Ա՛խ, ասես խարո՛յկ լինես՝ բոնկուած կանաչ բոցով,
Եւ Հեռուից քե՛զ եմ զգլում կարօտով կրակ սրտի.
Լցնում ես դաշտերն ամէն Հարազատ քո խշշոցով,
Իմ Հեռո՛ւ, Հեռո՛ւ, Հեռո՛ւ, նայիրեան դալա՛ր բարդի։

Իմ արտույտ-մանուկն աճա խաղում է քո շուաքում,
Քո փաւքին ե՛րգ է շրշում շրթներով կոկոն վարդի,
Ջո՛վ արա նրա կեանքին, Հօր նման զզուի՛ր անքուն,
Իմ Հեռո՛ւ, Հեռո՛ւ, Հեռո՛ւ, նայիրեան դալա՛ր բարդի։

Ես երգիչ Հրի՛, սրի՛, շատ շունե՛մ քո սիրուց դատ,
Քեզ նման կանաչ կեանքով՝ քեզ համար եյած մարտի,
Կը մեռնեմ, միայն թէ դու դարերում ազա՛տ խշշաս,
Իմ Հեռո՛ւ, Հեռո՛ւ, Հեռո՛ւ, նայիրեան դալա՛ր բարդի։

Green Poplar of Nairi

You sway and swing in your emerald cloak,
And shadow the road to the green fields of my childhood,
Your call rings deep in the rooms of my heart,
My faraway, faraway, faraway green poplar of Nairi.

A green poplar caught in a green flame;
With all the fire of longing I caress you from afar,
You fill the fields with a rustle entirely your own,
My faraway, faraway, faraway green poplar of Nairi.

My happy child plays here under your shade,
And with his tender rose lips, sings a song to you,
Bring coolness to his heart, stand gently over him like a sleepless
                                                                father,
My faraway, faraway, faraway green poplar of Nairi.

I sing of fire and battle, desire only your love,
I take up arms for you, with a life green as yours;
I will die that you may always breathe free,
My faraway, faraway, faraway green poplar of Nairi.

Nairi is the ancient Armenian name for Armenia.

Գէորգ Էմին

Gevork Emin

1915–

Սիամանթոյի Աղօթքը

«Ո՞վ յղացաւ այս միտքը դիւական՝
Մասիսը ճերմակ,
Մասիսը անբիծ
Այս լայն աշխարհում դնել այն տեղո'ւմ,
Ուր դար ու դարեր
Պիտի արիւնեն լանջե'րը նրա
Եւ գագա'թն անդամ.

Ո՞վ միտք յղացաւ
Դժոխք արարել
Եդեալ ու չեդեալ դրախտի տեղում՝
Արարատ լեռան Հովանու ներքոյ, —
Երկրի փոխարէն
Մեզ տալով մի հի'ն, ունակո'խ ճամբայ,
Հողի տեղ՝ չոր քա'ր,
Ջրի տեղ՝ արի'ւն...

Ո՞վ միտք յղացաւ
Դեռ մեր պատմութեան վաղ արշալոյսին
Այս արարչագործ,
Հին ժողովրդի
Գլուխը դնել մի հարեւանի՝
(Բիրտ Պարսկաստանի)
Արնոտ սրի տակ,
Միւսի աչով՝
(Բիւզանդիոյ խաչով)
Պահանջելով, որ նա... ծախսի՝ հոգին,
Եթէ ուզում է մարմինը վրկե'լ...

Եւ եթէ դարերն
Անգո'ր են եղել նրան ազատել,
Եւ եթէ դալիք
Դարերն անգո'ր են ազատել նրան,
Եւ հրա'շքն է լոկ
Չնա'րն անհնար,
Տէ'ր, տո'ւր ինձ Մովսէս մարգարէի պէս
Հանե'լ ու տանե'լ ցեղն իմ հալածուած
Այս Հայաստանի'ց, —

Siamanto's Prayer

Who conceived the idea, past praying for,
To fix on
Massis, white,
Spotless Massis?
In all the wide world in that place,
Age after age,
Blood has been let
On those slopes,
Even that peak.

Who conceived the idea
Of fashioning up hell
In this our land, real or imagined heaven
Under the shield of Ararat?
Yes, instead of country
Giving us a familiar old road,
Instead of land, dry rocks,
Instead of water, blood?

Who conceived the idea,
While yet in the early dawn of our history,
Of placing the head of this fecund
Venerable race
Under the bloody sword
Of a neighbor
—Bloody Persia,
And at the same time
—By dint of the Byzantine cross—
Demand that she sell her soul
If she choose to save her body?

And if the ages
Have been powerless to save her,
And if ages now rising
Should be powerless to save her,
And miracle itself be the only
Way out of the impossible,
Then, Lord, let me like the prophet Moses
Uproot and lead away my tormented race
From this Armenia—

Ո՛չ,
Մահատանի՛ց,
Ո՛չ,
Քարաստանի՛ց,
Դեպի ապահով, ուրի՛շ մի եզերք.
(Կա՞յ այդպիսի տեղ...)
Ցե՛դն իմ մշտատեև —
Նրա սե՛րմը նոր,
Արմատնե՛րը հին,
Վեպ, կոթող ու երգ...

Տո՛ւր պերճաբանիս
Թլուատութի՛ւնը նրա մոգական,
Եւ սո՛ւրը նրա՝
Աղբիւր հանելու հանդիպած քարից.
Եւ գալագա՛նը՝
Ծեղքելու Կարմիր Ծո՛վը մեր բախտի.
(Լացի՛ ու արեա՛ն...)
Թեկուզեւ Մովսէս մարգարէի պէս
Իմ մա՛հը գտնեմ,
Օտար հո՛ղ մտնեմ,
Այդ երանելի ափին չհասա՛ծ,
Բաղձալի սեմի՛ն նրա փակ դռան...

Տէ՛ր,
Զե՞ս լսում դու,
Կարմիր լուրերը ջարդի ու արեան...»

Ա՛խ, Այս Մասի՛սը

Ա՛խ, այս Մասի՛սը...

Որից փափկո՛ւմ են սրտերը բոլոր,
Երբ ինքը... քա՛ր է.

Որ ջերմացնո՛ւմ է սրտերը մոլոր,
Երբ ինքը... սա՛ռն է.

Yes,
From this charnel house,
Yes, from this rock-littered land
To another, safer shore.
(Is there really such a place?)
O my ever-enduring people!
New seed,
Old roots,
Now a story, now a song, a shrine.

Give the mellifluous rhetorician
The magic spell of his lisp,
Give him his sword
That he may strike water from the rocks near by;
Give him his staff
That he may cross the Red Sea of our fate
—Of tears and blood.
Though like the prophet Moses
I meet my death,
And enter on an alien land
Before I reach that beatific place
And the longed-for threshold of its closed door

Lord,
Dost Thou not hear
The red tidings—blood and massacre?

Ah, this Massis

Ah, this Massis,

Which mellows all hearts
Though itself a rock;

Which warms stray hearts
When itself is cold;

Որ աշխարհներից հեռավոր-հեռու
Բոլոր հայերին այստե'ղ է բերում,
Երբ ինքն... այստե'ղ էլ...

Միաբանութեան քարո'զ է կարդում
Աշխարհում ցրուած հայերին անտուն,
Երբ որ... կիսուա'ծ է.

Որ, մե'ծ սիրոյ պէս,
Ոչ հեռանո'ւմ է,
Ոչ էլ գալի'ս է...

Ա'խ, այս Մասի'սը։

Which brings all dispersed
Armenians home,
When itself is not here;

Preaches the sermon of unity
To the world-scattered homeless Armenians,
When itself is split in two;

Which like great love,
Neither drifts away
Nor draws near,

Ah, this Massis . . .

Մարօ Մարգարեան

Maro Markarian

1915–

Սրտիդ Վնաս Են

Սրտիդ վնաս են բարձրութիւնները,
Դու ապրիր խաղաղ ստորոտում.
Չխնի չերտեր են ու ցուրտ է վերը,
Դժուար է շնչել բարձր օդում.
Ինչի համար են այս մղումները
Եւ կատարների ծարաւը խենթ.
Եւ կայծակների քմահաճ դերը,
Ու վեր ելնելու հաչիչ ու տենդ:
Եւ ինչ են անում այն կատարները
Սառոյցների մէջ արձանացած
Ի ցոյց աշխարհին քարացած վերը,
Հնար էլ յուսեն նայելու ցած:
Եւ ի՞նչ են առել ամպերը իրար,
Կուտակուել սեւ-սեւ ու որոտում,
Սրտիդ վնաս են մեծ-մեծ բաները,
Մեծանուննները, մեծարանքները,
Դու ապրիր խաղաղ ստորոտում:

Դու Մի Բուռ . . .

Դու մի բուռ, մի ափ,
Դու մի սրտի չափ.
Դու սրտի պէս լայն,
Դու սրտի պէս խոր
Հայրենի իմ հող.
Ակունք բարիքի,
Բոյրի ու բերքի,
Խտացած իմ սէր,
Իմ հրաշք երկիր.
Դու մի բուռ, մի ափ,
Դու մի սրտի չափ:

The Heights are Harmful

The heights are harmful to your heart:
Live below, in the peaceful lowlands;
The snow is drifted high and it's cold up there,
It's hard to breathe thin mountain air.
And why all this striving,
The mad thirst for summits,
For the whimsies of lightning,
And all this frenzied climbing?
For what are these peaks,
Statues chiseled in ice,
Petrified somewhere in the clouds,
On display to the world below,
And no longer able to look down?
What are the clouds about, up there,
Gathering darkly and thundering?
The big words are harmful to your heart,
The great names, the high respects—
Live below here, in the peaceful lowlands.

The Size of a Heart

You are
A palm, a hand
The size of a heart,
You are
Broad as a heart
And as deep,
My homeland.
You are
Precious gems of good,
Of fragrance, of fertility;
You are
My distillation of love,
My miraculous land,
You are
The size of a heart,
A palm, a hand.

Սիլվա Կապուտիկեան

Silva Gaboudikian

1919–

Սիրոյ երգեր

1

Թէ ես չե՛մ սիրում, չե՛մ սիրում քեզ,
Ինչո՞ւ է ձմեռն այսքան գարո՛ւն,
Չոռան արբեր՝ այսքան այլո՛ւմ,
Անիւսս երկինքը՝ այսքան անհո՛ւն,
Թէ ես չեմ սիրում, չեմ սիրում քեզ:

Թէ դու չե՛ս սիրում, չե՛ս սիրում ինձ,
Հապա ինչո՞ւ են ձեր փողոցում
Այդքան սիրո՛վ ինձ ճամբայ բացում
Անցորդնե՛ր, տնե՛ր, մայթեր ու ճիւն,
Թէ դու չես սիրում, չես սիրում ինձ:

Ու թէ չենք սիրում մենք իրարու,
Ինչո՞ւ են աստղերն այսքան անթիւ,
Այսքան գեղեցի՛կ գիշեր ու տիւ,
Աշխարհը այսքան հա՛շտ ու ագնիւ,
Եթէ չենք սիրում ենք իրարու...

2

Հպարտ, բիւրեղեայ քո ձագկամանում
Ահով նուիրած իմ ձադիկները
Օրերով անջո՛ւր, անջո՛ւր են մնում:

Ու կաթիլ-կաթիլ՝ թոշնած թերթերը
Արցունքներիս պէս ընկնո՛ւմ են նկուն
Գրասեղանիդ սաւը ապակուն...

3

Երբ Դուք ծխում էք Ձեր գլանակը,
Թւում է նրա կրա՛կի մէջ
Իմ էութիւնից ինչ-որ մի բա՛ն կայ,
Որ մոխրանում է այնտեղ անվերջ:
Դուք ներս էք քաշում հոգուս կրակը,
Որ ցրէք մի պաշ ճանճրոյթը ցուրտ:

Լուռ ծխո՛ւմ էք Դուք վառ գլանակը
Ու մնացորդը նետո՛ւմ անփոյթ...

Love Songs

1

If I don't love you, and I don't love you,
Why is winter then so much like spring,
And winter's sun so brightly hot,
And the lowering sky so clear,
If I don't love you, and I don't love you.

If you don't love me, and you don't love me,
Then why is it that on your street
Passersby make way with so much kind concern,
And the houses, too, and the walks, the snow—
If you don't love me, and you don't love me.

And if we do not love each other,
Then why are there so many stars,
So much beauty in the night and day,
And so much at peace the world, so gentle—
If we do not love each other.

2

In your proud crystal vase,
The flowers I'd presented in high esteem
Remain unwatered for days on end,

And, one by one, the withered leaves,
Fall like my tears, humiliated,
On the cold glass of your desk.

3

When you puff on your cigarette
It always seems that in its fiery coal
There is something of my very being
That burns up there, as well.
You inhale the fire of my soul
To while away, for a time, cold tedium.

You puff on your cigarette silently,
And heedlessly cast off the butt.

4

Ասում էի «գնա՛, գնա՛», բայց դէ՛ ինչո՞ւ դու գնացիր,
Ասում էի «էլ մի՛ մնայ», բայց դու ինչո՞ւ չմնացիր.
Աչքերիս մէջ դողն արցունքի՝ ասում էի «Հաւատա՛ ինձ»,
Դու աչքերի՛ս հաւատայիր, խօսքիս ինչո՞ւ հաւատացիր...

5

Արի՛, արի՛, արի՛,
Թեկուզ վերջի՛ն անգամ,
Թեկուզ քայլով դժկամ,
Միայն արի՛, արի՛։

Թեկուզ անսէ՛ր, անսի՛րտ,
Թեկուզ հեգնող ու խիստ,
Թեկուզ խայթող ու բիրտ,
Միայն արի՛, արի՛։

Թեկուզ բերես դու ինձ
Մի նո՛ր դալի կսկից,
Թեկուզ ուրի՛շ գրկից,
Միայն արի՛, արի՛...

6

Թափառում ենք փողոցներում՝
Ես քո՛ սիրով, դու՝ ուրիշի,
Այրւո՛ւմ ենք մենք հրդեհներում՝
Ես քո հրով, դու՝ ուրիշի։

Կարօտում ենք, խնդում, տխրում՝
Ես քո՛ խօսքով, դու՝ ուրիշի,
Սուզւում քա՛ղցր երազներում՝
Ես քո՛ տեսքով, դու՝ ուրիշի։

Է՜հ, ի՛նչ արած, բախտը խոտով
Թող աշխարհում մեզ չլքի,
Միայն ապրենք մենք սիրելո՛վ՝
Թեկուզ ես՝ քե՛զ, դու՝ ուրիշի՛...

4

I said "go, go away," but why did you leave?
I said "stay no more," but why didn't you stay?
My eyes, trembling with tears, said "believe in me,"
You should have believed my eyes—why did you believe my words?

5

Come, come, come,
Though for the last time,
Though with a reluctant step,
Come, only do come.

Though loveless and heartless,
Though harsh and sarcastic,
Though rough and stinging,
Come, only do come,

Though perhaps you bring
Me the pain of some new harm,
Though from another's embrace,
Come, only do come.

6

We wander the streets,
I with your love, and you with another's—
We burn with such fires,
I for you, and you for another.

We long for, laugh, become sad,
I at your words, you at another's,
We sleep and fall into wonderful dreams,
I with your looks, you with another's.

Well, so what, perverse luck—
Let the world forget that we were;
But, oh, that we had lived in love,
Though I with you, and you with another.

Լիլիթ

«Եւա» էին հնչում նրա շրթները,
սակայն «Լիլիթ» էր արձագանքում
նրա հոգին։
Ալ. Խաչակեան

Նախամարդու գոյգ քարերից բունկուած պեծ
Ու նեռնէն կրակների ծփա՛նք դու պերճ.
Ի սկզբանէ աննիւթ, անմար, անհուն, անվերջ,
Լիլիթ, Լիլիթ։

Դու՝ աշխարհի աչքից դարեր գաղտնեգրուած,
Հոգու թաքուն կարօտներից հրահրուած,
Քո գաղտնութեամբ առաւել քա՛ղցր, առաւել գա՛նձ,
Լիլիթ, Լիլիթ։

Սրտերի մէջ դու՝ տօնական օր ու անկիւն,
Դու՝ խոյանքի, խինդի, խանդի, տենդի ակունք,
Դու ես՝ մարմի՛ն, դու ես՝ թեւե՛ր, դու ես՝ անկում,
Լիլիթ, Լիլիթ։

Շուրջը՝ հողէ, ու հաց, ու հոգս — իսկ դու ցնորք,
Դու՝ միայն փայլ, ամէն օր՝ այլ, ամէն օր՝ նոր,
Կանչող, տանջող, այրւող, այրող — ու յոգնեցնո՛ղ,
Լիլիթ, Լիլիթ։

Այնտեղ սենեակ գողտր ու տաքուկ — ու դու՝ փողոց,
Այնտեղ օջախ — դու՝ անհանգիստ խարոյկի բոց,
Այնտեղ անդորր — դու՝ անդադրում խռովք ու խոց,
Լիլիթ, Լիլիթ։

Այնտեղ Եւան — դու՝ անվալեր ու անստոյգ,
Դու՝ հրեղէն արեան չարաչ ու՝ անպտո՛ւղ,
Մենա՛կ, մենա՛կ, երկրից, երկնից, դրախտից՝ դո՛ւրս,
Լիլիթ, Լիլիթ։

Lilith

> His lips sounded "Eve," but his soul echoed "Lilith."
>
> A. Issahakian

A spark kindled from the twin rocks of early man
Are you, an undulating vision of neon lights—
From the beginning an other being, eternal, infinite, endless,
Lilith, Lilith.

You, the secret shielded from the eyes of centuries,
Burning in the soul's most hidden fire,
You in your mystery are most sweet, most precious,
Lilith, Lilith.

You are a celebration clinging in a fastness of our hearts,
A wellspring of desire, fervor, aspiration, joy,
You are the body and the wing and the fall,
Lilith, Lilith.

Everywhere around us are earth, bread, concern, while you remain
                                                        the dream,
You, always a brightness, always different, every day new,
Alluring, tormenting, burning—the fire that consumes us all,
Lilith, Lilith.

There is a secret, intimate room and you are the path to it,
A hearth is there, and you are its restless blazing,
A calm is there, and you its unceasing torment,
Lilith, Lilith.

And there is Eve, while you remain invalid, indistinct,
Fruitless, but of our blood, you, the fire's roar,
Alone, alone—cast from earth, from heaven, from paradise,
Lilith, Lilith.

Հրաչեայ Յովհաննիսեան

Hrachia Hovhanissian

1920–

Անձրևեն Անցնի՛

Անձրևեն անցնի՝ գիւղից դո՛ւրս գամ,
Հանդերն ընկնեմ, թափառե՛մ,
Աղբիւրներով աքանչանամ,
Ծաղիկները փայփայեմ:

Հովը դէմքիս ցօղե՛ր ցանի,
Հովից ծառերն օրօրուե՛ն,
Գերուեմ խաղով ծիածանի,
Կածաններում մոլորուեմ:

Ընկնե՛մ սար, ձոր, մտնեմ անտառ,
Արբեմ օղով չինչ ու թարմ,
Լեռներին տամ իղձերս վառ,
Ձեփիւրներին սէ՛րս տամ:

Մի շո՛ղ, մի քո՛յր, մի գո՛յն տանեմ,
Ամէն մէկից, բոլորի՛ց,
Ման գամ, իմ ողջ կարօտն առնեմ
Հայրենական իմ հողից:

Տանեմ մի՛ գոյն, մի՛ քոյր, մի՛ շող՝
Երգերիս մէջ ամբարեմ,
Ու երգիս հետ, անո՛ւշ իմ հող,
Քո սուածը քե՛զ բերեմ:

Ասո՛ւմ են, Կարապը ...

Ասում են՝ կարապը մի՛ անգամ է սիրում,
Լոկ մէկկի՛ն է սիրում, սիրում է առյաւէ՛տ,
Ու երբ մահն է գալիս՝ լույս թևերն է փռում,
Լոկ մի՛ անգամ երգում, մեռնում է երգի՛ հետ...

Սիրելիս, ես կեանքում քեզ շատ եմ որոնել
Ու գտել մի՛ անգամ ուսիրել ձերմագին,
Եւ միայն այսքանով նման է սէրը մեր
Սիրահար կարապի սրտառուչ լեգենդին:

When the Rain Passes

Once the rain passes, I will leave the village
And go out running in the fields,
Become lost among the springs,
Caressing the flowers.

The wind will carry the dew to my face,
The trees begin swaying in the wind,
And delighted by the rainbow's play I
Will get lost among the lanes.

I will enter the woods, wander among
The hills and valleys, drunk with the pure taste of the air,
Offer my bright imaginings to the mountains
And my love to the gentle breeze.

I will take away with me a ray, a fragrance, a hue
From each one and from all—
Roam, fill the longings tumbling in me,
Longings bound with the earth of my native land.

I will take away with me a ray, fragrance, a hue,
And gather them into my songs,
And with these songs, my endearing homeland,
Leave with you what you have given me.

The Swan

They say the swan loves only once,
Loves only once, loves forever;
And when death comes, the swan spreads its wings,
Sings only once, and dies with its one song.

My darling, through all my life I searched for you,
And once I found you always loved you;
And in this alone is our love akin
To the noble legend of the swan.

Այսքանո՛վ, սիրելիս։ Քանզի մենք իրարու
Փնտռել ենք ու գտել այնպիսի՛ յոյսերով,
Գտել ենք՝ յաւիտեա՛ն սիրելու, ապրելո՛ւ,
Ցաւիտեա՛ն երգելու թովչանքը մեր սիրոյ։

Հեքեաթը կարապի տխուր է վերջանում . . .
Բայց խո՛րն է խորհուրդը մարդկային մեր կեանքի —
Ես այն ա՛ն եմ սիրում, որ թեւերն է բանում
Անսովոր, անվայրէջ, անսահմա՛ն ճախրանքի։

Darling, only in this: we searched for
And found each other, with such hope,
And we found each other so to love forever,
Forever to live and sing the gentle beauty of our love.

The swan's tale ends unhappily,
Deep is the questing of our human life,
My love is for that love that opens up its untried
Wings and soars forever in a climeless place.

Վահագն Կարենց

Vahakn Garents

1924–

Երազներիս Համար

Երազներիս համար պարտական եմ ես ձեզ,
Արևամա՛ք ժայռեր՝
Իրար թիկնած խոժոռ,
Ճանապարհնե՛ր փոշոտ,
Փոշում կորած գառներ,
Երազներիս համար պարտական եմ ես ձեզ։

Պարտական եմ ես ձեզ երազների՛ս համար,
Ձե՛զ, քարեհասկ արտեր,
Քարե գետե՛ր անձայն,
Լեգենդ ու յուշ դարձած քարե՛ ցանկապատեր,
Պարտական եմ ես ձեզ երազներիս համար։

Երազներիս համար պարտական եմ ես ձեզ՝
Մառախուղնե՛ր ճերմակ
Բլուրներին իջած,
Մեռունինե՛ր անչար
Նստած պատերի տակ,
Երազներիս համար պարտական եմ ես ձեզ։

Պարտական եմ ես ձեզ երազներիս համար՝
Աշնան գիշերներին
Ինձնից թռա՛ծ հավքեր,
Անհետ կորա՛ծ երգեր
Զուռնա՛ծ գինևորների,
Պարտական եմ ես ձեզ երազներիս համար։

Երազներիս համար պարտական եմ ես ձեզ՝
Անիրական այգում
Իմ ծաղիկնե՛ր քրած,
Իմ ազջիկնե՛ր սիրած
Ուրիշների գրկում,
Երազներիս համար պարտական եմ ես ձեզ։

For my Dreams

I thank you for my dreams,
Sun-cracked rocks
That lean together sullenly,
Dusty roads,
Lambs lost in the dust—
I am thankful to you for my dreams.

I thank you for my dreams,
You, rock-growing fields,
Rock strewn, silent rivers,
Stone walls
Turned into legend and memory—
I am thankful to you for my dreams.

I thank you for my dreams,
White mists
Settled in hills,
Tired old men
Seated under the walls—
I am thankful to you for my dreams.

I thank you for my dreams,
The fowl that fluttered away from me
On autumn nights,
The soundless, vanished songs
Of martyred soldiers sacrificed—
I am thankful to you for my dreams.

I thank you for my dreams,
My flowers watered
In an unreal garden,
The girls I love
On the laps of others—
I am thankful to you for my dreams.

Ելի՛ր քեզնից ու Գնա՛

Ելի՛ր քեգնից ու գնա՛,
Գնա՛, քեգնից Հեռացի՛ր
Ելյութեան քո տունը
Միածանի՛ց կառուցիր․
Կակաչներից առուակի,
Վերջալույսի գույքերից,
Փետուրներից կոււնկի,
Ճամբորդների խոսքերից,
Խխունջներից ծովերի,
Չկնորսների ցանցերից,
Խրխինջներից ձիերի,
Խարույկների կայծերից։

Ելի՛ր քեգնից, ու գնա՛,
Դու Հեռացի՛ր քեզանից,
Ելյութեան քո տունը
Հիւսիր ճերմակ ամպերից․
Հիւսիր թաւի՛շ խոտերից,
Եղեգներից դետափի,
Լուսնի արծաթ շողերից,
Մամուռներից քարափի,
Հովիւրների երգերից,
Դայլայլներից Հաւքերի,
Անձրեւների ցօղերից,
Շշուկներից Հասկերի։

Հիւսի՛ր պատերը քո տան
Պարպած գինու շշերից,
Ու սրբատաշ, սրբատա՛շ
Նուրբ քարերից յուշերի,
Մայրամուտին երկարած
Ստուերների՛ց ծառերի,
Երամներից թեւ առած,
Քեգնից թռչո՛դ բառերի։
Դու Հեռացի՛ր քեզանից,
Ելի՛ր քեգնից ու գնա՛,
Որ լույեան քո տանից
Այս ադմուկը Հասկանաս։

Get Away from Your Self, Go

Get away from your self, go,
Remove your self from yourself
And go, build your house of silence
From the rainbow,
From the music of streams,
The glitter of twilight,
The feathers of cranes,
The words of travelers,
The snails of the sea,
The nets of fishermen,
The neigh of horses,
The sparks of bonfires.

Get away from your self, go,
Remove your self from yourself,
And go, weave your house of silence
From high clouds,
Velvet grass,
Canebrakes at the riverside,
The silver rays of the moon,
The moss on shorelines,
Songs of the shepherds,
The twitterings of fowl,
Mists of rain,
The rustling of cornstalks.

Fashion the walls of your house
From emptied bottles of wine
And the smoothly cut,
Delicate stones of memories;
From the treeshadows
Lengthening in twilight;
From the words that soared away
From you when you held forth in groups of friends,
Get away from your self, go,
Remove your self from yourself,
So that from your house of silence
You may hear and know this rich noise abroad.

Վահագն Դաւթեան

Vahakn Davtian

1922–

Սիրտս

Մի նուրբ ճնճաղիկ հոդից նոր եկած՝
Արցունքի մի շիթ՝ թերթերի մեջ թաց,
Մի ծիծեռնակի սրածեւ սլացք,
Ինչ-որ աղջկայ քնքո՛ւշ մի հայեացք,
Արևի մի շող բեկբեկուն ու տաք՝
Ու թրթռում ես, սի՛րտ իմ, կրծքիս տակ...։
Ի՞նչ ես դույիշում,
        չգիտե՛մ,
                բայց ես
Շնորհապա՛րտ եմ, սիրտ իմ, քեզ այնպե՛ս,
Որ դու կարող ես այդպես թրթռալ
Եւ որ խենթացած կարող ես դու լա՛լ,
Մի նուրբ ճնճաղկից, մի բեկո՛ր յուշից,
Դաշտերին իջած կապո՛յտ մշուշից,
Գարնան հալոցքից, հաւքի սլացքի՛ց,
Ինչ-որ աղջկայ քնքո՛ւշ հայեացքից։

My Heart

An intricate snowflake, delicate, new on the earth,
And a tear dropped among the wet leaves,
The flight of a sharp-winged swallow,
The glance of a gentle girl,
The sun's ray, softly bright and warm,
And you throb inside my breast, my heart,
What it is you remember
    I do not know,
    But I
Am so grateful, my heart,
That you can throb so,
And that though maddened, you can sob
For an intricate snowflake, a shred of memory,
The blue mist hovering over the fields,
The flight of a bird, the melting of spring,
For the glance of a gentle girl.

Արամ Արման

Aram Arman

1923–

Վերադարձի Գազէլ

Աշխարհ ամբողջ աշքերուս մէջ՝ հիմա գրկա'ծ կու գամ քեզի,
Արիւնս յորդ, բուռնքս պիրկ, ու սիրտս բա'ց կու գամ քեզի։

Անցեր եմ ես ամէ'ն ճամբով, տեսեր հազար մոլուցք ու կիրք,
Եւ անոնցմէ վերքե'ր առած, աշքերս թա'ց կու գամ քեզի։

Վեր է ժայթքեր իմ հոգին միշտ ու տիրացեր ոլորաններուն,
Բայց ոլորտի'դ համար անհաս՝ դլուխս ցա'ծ կու գամ քեզի։

Ես պոռտան եմ քու գաղթական, նետած հասակ մեծ դարուն հետ,
Ու այդ դարուն բունկումէն որպէս մէկ կա'յծ կու գամ քեզի։

Ընդունէ' զիս, երկիր իմ նոր՝ իմաստութեամբ ու կաթոգին, —
Հոկտեմբերիդ դրօշին տակ երդս պարզա'ծ կու գամ քեզի։

The Chant of the Returned Poet

With the whole world reflected in my eyes, I come to you,
My blood racing, my fists clenched, my heart open, I come to you.

I've traveled every road, seen passion and fury without end.
And wounded by passion and fury, in tears I come to you.

My soul has always soared up and reached the heights,
But unable to reach your heights, with my head bowed I come to you.

I am your immigrant poet, I have grown with the great spring;
As a spark caught from the fire of that spring, I come to you.

Accept me tenderly, my new country, and with wisdom—
I come to you singing my song, beneath your Octobrist flag.

Պարոյր Սևակ

Barouyr Sevak

1924–1971

Բարի իրիկուն

Արեգակն է թեքւում։
Կարճանում է օրը։
Եւ լեռները նորից երեկոյ են ծնում՝
Ստուերների տեսքով,
Որ մեծանում քիչ-քիչ
Ու թաղում են իրենց ծնող մօրը։

Պատահողմը՝
Ցենուած ռանաթափի վրայ,
Խոյանում է երկինք՝
Հաստատելով
Ժխտուած առասպելը համբարձումի։

Ցրտող օդում դանդաղ թխրտում է
Մի կտոր տաք մարմին,
Որ թռչուն է կոչւում։

Ինչ-որ կին է կանգնած խուլի դաշտի մէջ,
Եւ ուռների տակով անց է կենում
Երկրագնդի անտես այն առանցքը,
Որի երեւացող մասն է ինքը։

Առա՛նց յանցանքի մէջ բռնուելու,
Առա՛նց վկաների առկայութեան
Ինքըս մեղաւոր եմ ինձ ճանչում
Ու վախուորա՛ծ-քաշուա՛ծ մրմնջում եմ հեռուից,
Մրմնջում եմ արդէն ո՛չ թէ սրան,
Այլ այն մէկի՛ն՝ իմի՛ն, հեռաւորի՛ն.
—Բարի իրիկուն քեզ, ի՛մ մենաւոր...

Առաւօտ Լուսոյ

Առաւօտ լուսո՛յ,
Առաւօտ մի ջի՛նջ,
Ջի՛նջ, ինչպէս ... ուխի՛նչ,
Ջի՛նջ, սակայն դեռ պա՛ղ։

Good Evening

The sun slides down,
The day narrows to a close,
And again the mountains bear children,
Shadowshapes
That grow little by little
And bury their mothers.

The whirlwind
Leaning on its foot,
Soars up into the sky,
Confirming
The recanted legend of the Ascension.

In the chilling air, a small
Warm body, some say a bird,
Stumbles in flight.

A woman stands in an enclosed field,
And under her feet
The axis of the earth turns, unseen,
And unseen, forms a part of her.

Without being caught red-handed,
Without eyewitnesses present,
I see myself guilty;

And drawn by fear unto myself, I mumble from afar,
And I mumble now, not to that one,
But to this one—me, the remote one—
"Good evening, my solitary one . . . "

Morning Light

A morning of light,
A morning that's clean,
Clean like . . . nothing,
Clean, and yet still cold.

Ու ես անյապաղ
Անջատում եմ ինձ
Աշխարհից ծանոթ
Ու պարպում եմ ինձ,
Դարձնում մի անոթ,
Որ լոկ դատարկ է՜,
Այլ նաեւ անօղ:
Եւ ... նո՛ր աշխարհ եմ ստեղծում հիմա՝
Առայժմ եթէ ոչ ձեզ բոլորիդ,
Ապա գոնէ ի՛նձ, միայն ի՛նձ համար,
Որպէսզի նախ ե՛ս
Եւ հէնց ի՛նձ վրայ
Բժշկի նման փորձարկեմ կարգին,
Ու եթէ լինի այս անգամ սարքին՝
Նո՛ր միայն վատահ յանձնեմ ձե՛զ նաեւ,
Եւ ապրէք այնտեղ դուք մարդավայել:

Ես՝ պատրանագերծ,
Բայց եւ յուսագէն,
Այս դեռ անվաւեր ու նոր աշխարհում
էլ չե՛մ գբաղում ու չե՛մ գբաղուի
Ջեղածի վրայ եղածի թերին ի զո՛ւր քննելով,
Եղագի վրայ երեխայաբար անո՛նրջ դնելով,
Կեղծուած դրամով կեղծ բան գնելով,
Ոչ էլ ճարահատ ու միտումնօրէն
Մահանալու պէս անվերջ քնելով:

Ես՝ գարիծած արդէն,
Բայց դեռ անլուայ,
Հեղուկով մի կուզ,
Որ պարգեւում է ձնհան անխուսափ,
Նախ գովածնում եմ դէմքն իմ՝ հիանդի՛,
Իսկ յետոյ՝ ամէ՛ն տեսակ հիանդի՛

And immediately I
Detach myself
From the familiar world
And decant myself
As though from a vessel
That is not merely empty
But airless.
And
I create a different world,
If not now for all of you,
At least for me
And only me,
Because
I must probe first, like a doctor,
And satisfy myself that it has all turned out right;
Then and only then may I pass it on to you
Confidently,
So that you may live then
After the manner of all humankind.

I,
Stripped of dreams,
Am nevertheless armed with hope;
In this new and unauthenticated world
I no longer keep busy or busy myself
Criticizing
In. vain the flaws of something that doesn't exist,
And like a child
Superimposing longings
On dreams,
Buying fake things with counterfeit money,
Nor shall I be
Hopeless and inclined
To sleep forever once I am dead.

I,
Already awake,
But still unwashed,
With a handful of liquid,
A constant offer from the melting snow,
First to cool my face, this sick man's face,
And then the faces of all other patients,

Մա՞րդ լինի, երկի՞ր, թէ՞ հաւատ, — մէ՛կ է:
Զովացնում նրանց ամէնքի դէմքը՝
Իմ ամենաբուժ մատների հեռքը
Անչինչ թողնելով սրա ու նրա
Դեռ գոց կոպերի,
Դեռ փակ շուրթերի,
Տակաւին քնկոտ երեսի վրայ:

Ու բոլորի՛դ մէջ,
Անխտիր բոլո՛ր-բոլո՛ր-բոլորի՛դ,
Ինչ-որ սիրելի մի բան եմ գտնում,
Սիրելու ինչ-որ արժանի մը բան,
Որ հաւանաբար
Ա՛յն ժամանակ է ստեղծուել արդէն,
Երբ հին չորս ոտքից երկուսը
Անդարձ
Մենք կորցրեցինք...

Եւ վեհ բարձունքից աններողութեան
Ես, քարի նման, վար եմ թալալում՝
Հասնելով փափուկ ա՛յն ստորոտին,
Որից քիչ անդին
Ձահիճն է ապրում
Իր յաւերժական ինքնածին կեանքով,
Եւ, քարի լեզուով, ասում եմ. «Այբ Բեն»,
Այսինքն՝ «Արեգակ»,
Կամ՝ «Եղիցի լոյս»...

Man, the world, or faith, they're all the same.
I cool their faces,
Leaving the trace
Of my all-curing fingers
On one thing and another,

On still sealed eyelids,
On still closed lips,
On faces still heavy with sleep.
And
In all of you,
In all, in all of you
Without distinction,
I find something endearing,
Something deserving love
Which perhaps existed
When we lost two of our four feet
Irretrievably,

And
From the lofty heights
Of this perfection
I tumble, like a rock,
Reaching that gentle slope
Beyond which, only a little distance away,
Lies the marshland
In eternal, self-creating life,
And
In the language of rocks, of simple elements, I say "A, B, C,"
That is,
"Sun"
Or
"Let there be light"

Index of Titles and First Lines

Titles of poems are in roman type and first lines in italics.

A Birthday Melody   41
Across the hoary crest of Ararat   215
A Gentle Sleep   149
A Handful of Ash   225
Ah, give me a gentle sleep   149
Ah, It Came to Mind   305
Ah, this Massis   331
Alas, you were a great and beautiful mansion   225
A morning of light   369
An intricate snowflake, delicate, new on the earth   361
Argument between the Sky and Earth   81
A spark kindled from the twin rocks of early man   345
At daybreak he walked up the gallows   253
A Vision of Death   269
Awake, you who are saved by His blood   47
A young girl tells me   263

Brothers, they lie when they say you cannot tame a peacock   75

Come, come, come   343
Come, let's go into the garden and sit among the roses   89
Come, nightingale, leave our garden   117
Compassion   263
Complaint   51
Conception grand and marvelous   33
Cradle Song   117

David of Sassoun   161
Don't you cry, bulbul, don't you droop   145
During the night I slept, but my heart stayed awake   75

Entirely draped in a black silk, unlustrous gown   221
Even now, brothers, shall we still be silent, shall we   119
Every moment with sorrowing love I say farewell   255
Every morning at daybreak   63

Farewell Song   255
Fatherland   267
For my Dreams   355
Freedom   107
From Ravenna   215
From the day that God, serene and unconstrained   107
From your royal sleep, wake   93

Get away from your self, go   357
Good Evening   369
Green Poplar of Nairi   325

Her eyes gaze   41
How can we know the Creator's unknowable mysteries   159
However much I wish to climb to your heights   153
How often have I said don't love the rose, it carries thorns   73
How that moment was like a dying icon lamp   269
Hrazdan, river of my homeland   103

I am the eye and you the light, my soul, without light the eye is dark   73
I am young and so are you, and now is the time for love   75
If I don't love you, and I don't love you   341
I love my sweet Armenia's sun-flavored speech   267
I made my life into a village green, walked on by everyone   159
Impromptu   315
In my dreams a ewe   159
In the mist of this present scene   253
In the Woods   323
In your proud crystal vase   341
I placed my heart inside an ancient oak   315
I said "go, go away," but why did you leave   343
I thank you for my dreams   355
I was one of the birds who didn't seek for grain on the ground   73
I wish I were a hut   243
I'll not cry "alas" to all this world so long as you're the soul of my life   97

Joined with our Land   311

Lilith   345
Lion-Mher of fable and legend   161
Little lake, speak up, why are you silent   129
Lord of Peace   29
Love Song   57
Love Songs   341

Index / 376

Moon, you boast and say, "I bring forth light to a dark world" 75
Morning Light 369
My Death 141
My Heart 361
My Land 153

Niagara, Niagara, you crash down 315
Night 285

Oak and Eagle 315
O holy virgin, pillar of light, cloud of shade 35
O just and righteous God 51
Old Stork 293
O Lord of peace, help me to turn away 29
Oh may this journey be endless 319
O mild breeze, all through the early morning 113
O my almond blossom, you bloomed and became delicious 77
O my high, roaming moon, where do you go through the broad night 75
O my little one, shall I ever conquer your bosom 75
O my mother, sun and remote moon 311
Once the rain passes, I will leave the village 349
Only a rose on my bier when I die 297
On this cold night, forsaking my work, I come to your door 77
Oriental Bath 233
Over the stream 217

Pillar of Light 35
Prayer One, from the *Book of Lamentations* 43

Quatrains 159

Remembrance 133
Requiem 297

She has a face, shall it be said, like the moon 289
Siamanto's Prayer 329
Since I was born of a woman, I will not confess to a priest 73
Sister 289
Snow-wrapped mountains and blue lakes 267
So beautiful, tender, so gentle 57
Song 93
Song of Love (HOVNATON) 89
Song of Love (TELKURANTSI) 69
Song to Weeping, and to the Owner of a New-built House and Garden 63

Sounds of lamentation 43
Spring 113
Suddenly I saw a face, radiant with color 69
Sun-flavored Speech 267
Swallow (DODOKHIAN) 125
Swallow (VAHOUNI) 301

The Armenians' Grief 159
The beautiful one is always she who walked past you one day 221
The Birth of Vahakn, King of Armenia 33
The Chant of the Returned Poet 365
The Flickering Lamp 231
The Beautiful Ones 221
The Gallows 253
The Glass 281
The Hanoum 221
The heights are harmful to your heart 337
The Hut 243
The inner door of the green-domed bath opens slowly 233
The King has come to earth 25
The Lamb 277
The misted rose has drawn a veil 39
The Newsboy 259
The news was brought that my beloved had become a nun 73
There are birds that outlive men 301
There were small clouds in the woods 323
The sad days, like winter, come and go 137
The Size of a Heart 337
The sky and the earth are brothers 81
The sky is turbulent, turbulent the earth 33
The sun slides down 369
The swallow is building a nest 133
The Swan 349
The whole night through the poplars 285
The woodland shook, it thundered with laughter 277
The world's a window—I'm weary of so many windows 99
They are the mighty children of the fields 231
They Come and Go 137
They say the swan loves only once 349
This Endless Journey 319
This is a night for feast and triumph 231
This lifeless glass winks at me 281
This whole cold night through till dawn I sat spinning two rows of yarn 77
Thoughts 73

Tillers 31
Today I read from Leyli-Mejnoun   305
Today the flock passed through the heavy sky for the last time   293
To my Native Home   273
Tonight I had a sweet dream   273

Vartan's Song   119
Vartavar   39

We wander the streets   343
We were peaceful as our mountains   315
When the pallid angel of death   141
When the Rain Passes   349
When you puff on your cigarette   341
Where Does the Stone Lie   215
Who conceived the idea, past praying for   329
Why, why did you fall in love with me?   249
With the whole world reflected in my eyes, I come to you   365

You are   337
Your heart is my white temple, and your breasts are holy lanterns   73
You small, fair boy with your eyes like lakes   259
You sway and swing in your emerald cloak   325

Aram Tolegian is Emeritus Dean, East Los Angeles College, and has taught English and Comparative Literature at the University of Southern California, California State University (Los Angeles), Pepperdine University, and other institutions. He received his B.A. from the University of California (1936), and his M.A. and Ph.D. from the University of Southern California (1941, 1960).

The manuscript was prepared for publication by W. L. Wienner. The book was designed by Gary Gore. The typeface for the English text and display is Baskerville, based on an original design by John Baskerville in the eighteenth century. The typeface for the Armenian text and display is Armenian Barz. The book is bound in Holliston Mills Kenneth cloth over binder's boards. Manufactured in the United States of America.